Contents

KU-726-406

Contents

How to Complete Your UCAS Application

2014 entry

25th edition

trotman | **t**

Getting into guides

Getting into Art & Design Courses, 8th edition
Getting into Business & Economics Courses, 10th edition
Getting into Dental School, 8th edition
Getting into Engineering Courses, 2nd edition
Getting into Law, 9th edition
Getting into Medical School: 2014 entry, 18th edition
Getting into Nursing & Midwifery, 1st edition
Getting into Oxford & Cambridge: 2014 entry, 16th edition
Getting into Physiotherapy Courses, 6th edition
Getting into Psychology Courses, 9th edition
Getting into Veterinary School, 9th edition

How to Complete Your UCAS Application: 2014 Entry

This 25th edition published in 2013 by Trotman Publishing, an imprint of Crimson Publishing Ltd, Westminster House, Kew Road, Richmond, Surrey TW9 2ND

Foreword by Steve Jeffree © Steve Jeffree
Updated by UCAS and Beryl Dixon

© Trotman Publishing 2013, 2012, 2011, 2010, 2009, 2008, 2007

Editions 19–24 published by Trotman Publishing in 2007, 2008, 2009, 2010, 2011, 2012
Editions 1–18 published by Trotman & Co. Ltd

Previously published as *How to Complete Your UCCA/PCAS Form*
Screenshots from UCAS Apply, Figures 1 and 2, UCAS Tariff tables © UCAS. Reproduced with kind permission of UCAS

British Library Cataloguing in Publication Data
A catalogue record for this book is available from the British Library

ISBN 978 1 90604 195 3

Typeset by IDSUK (DataConnection) Ltd
Printed and bound in the UK by TJ International Ltd, Padstow, Cornwall

Foreword

First decision: where to begin?

Congratulations! You've made an important decision to apply for a degree course. But where can you get information about turning that decision into a reality? With so many choices and so many combinations of subjects, some of which may be new to you, you need some help in deciding what and where to study.

As well as supporting the whole applications process each year, UCAS – the Universities and Colleges Admissions Service – helps thousands of potential students find the right study match. We believe that giving you access to as much information as possible at this stage in your application is vital in ensuring that you make the right decisions about your future study.

The research you do and the advice you get can all provide a valuable insight into which is the perfect course for you. Our UCAS search tool on www.ucas.com is the definitive source of information on the courses and the institutions that could be an option for you. We advise you to look closely at this information, be realistic about the institutions' entry requirements and, if possible, make a visit to the universities and colleges that you are interested in. Remember, you will potentially be spending three or four years there, so it needs to feel like the right place.

You'll find www.ucas.com has all the information you need to help you make your application. There are downloads, guides, how-to videos and social media, as well as plenty of tips and blogs from students, parents and advisers. Have a look round – and talk to us on Facebook or Twitter if you've got any questions.

The actual process of applying is simple and is all online. You can find everything you need to know about it in this book, but if you have a question that remains unanswered, contact us online or call one of our experts on 0871 468 0 468.

Best of luck with your research and application!

Steve Jeffree

Chief Operating Officer, UCAS

Introduction

This book is intended to be a guide for anyone wanting to gain a place on a UK higher education course. In 2012, 464,910 people were accepted onto approximately 37,000 courses of higher education at over 300 UK universities and colleges. For 2013, by the main application deadline of 15 January 2013, 558,898 had already applied – an increase of 18,825 or 3.5% in the number of applications (2.8% for UK applicants). More, however, may apply during the course of the year, since every year many people apply after the 'advisory' January deadline (last year UCAS received over 110,000 applications after the January deadline had expired). All of these potential students had to complete UCAS applications to try to gain their university or college place.

The job of UCAS

With very few exceptions, every application to a full-time higher education course, whether a degree, a course leading to a degree, a foundation degree, Higher National Diploma (HND) or Diploma of Higher Education (DipHE), must be made through UCAS. UCAS manages and monitors the flow of applications to universities and colleges and their decisions to would-be entrants. UCAS acts as the intermediary between students and their intended universities and colleges, providing lists of available courses and the means by which prospective students can apply for them.

As well as handling initial applications, UCAS also offers two valuable services when the summer exam results come out – Adjustment and Clearing. Both services are designed to help students whose results are not what they expected (Adjustment for those with better grades and Clearing for those whose grades are lower). Both services are described in Chapter 10.

UCAS offers a considerable amount of help to higher education applicants on its website, www.ucas.com, where you can:

- use the UCAS search tool to research the courses offered by different universities and colleges using a number of variables such as qualification (degree, HND, etc.), subject, university or college, or geographical area
- find out the entry requirements for courses, including grades and Tariff points and any additional requirements

- find out more about each course, including its content, mode of delivery and method of assessment, all in the course details
- link to any higher education institution's website
- make an online application to your chosen university courses through Apply
- log in to Track to follow the progress of your application
- link to Extra to find an additional course to apply to, if you have used all your choices and are not holding any offers
- get information about financing your studies
- go through Clearing if you have your results but no offers.

Of course, applying through UCAS is no guarantee of a place on a higher education course. Every year, a number of individuals apply but do not get offered places. But this is the starting point of a whole new phase of your life, whether you take a higher education course or an alternative learning route. Either pathway can lead to the personal fulfilment and independence that an interesting and worthwhile career can provide.

Using this guide

This book is divided into three parts. A brief outline of the content and purpose of each part is given below.

Part I. In the think tank

Before you make a UCAS application, it is important that you thoroughly research all your higher education options. The first part of this guide gives you a number of ideas about the areas that need detailed consideration before you can be confident of making the right higher education course choices for you. Its six chapters guide you through the decision-making process, helping you to find answers to key questions such as these.

- Is higher education the right option for me? (See Chapter 1.)
- How will a degree or higher diploma fit in with my career plans? (See Chapter 2.)
- How will I afford it? (See Chapter 3.)
- How do I choose what and where to study? (See Chapters 4 and 5.)
- Will I meet the entry requirements? (See Chapter 6.)

You need to be ready to explain and justify your decision. Admissions tutors (who read your UCAS application and who may interview you) will want to know why you have applied for a place on their particular course. At the end of most chapters there is a 'Resources' section suggesting points of reference that can be accessed in your school or college library or local careers centre. Ask advisers for help in finding the most up-to-date materials.

Part II. The admissions procedure: applications, interviews, offers and beyond

Once you have decided which courses to apply for, the second part of the book gives you an overview of the entire admissions procedure. It works through the whole process, answering key questions like these.

- When do I submit my application? (See Chapter 7.)
- How do universities and colleges communicate their offers to me? (See Chapter 7.)
- How do I accept or decline offers? (See Chapter 7.)
- What about non-standard applications? (See Chapter 8.)
- How can I maximise my chances if I'm called for interview? (See Chapter 9.)
- What happens on exam results day? (See Chapter 10.)
- How do I use Clearing? (See Chapter 10.)

Part III. Using Apply to submit your UCAS application

Part III covers the technicalities of filling in and submitting your UCAS application online using Apply, taking you through the process step by step and offering helpful advice and tips on how to avoid the pitfalls.

Staying on the straight and narrow: timetable for advanced-level students

If you stick to the timetable, the whole process of applying to higher education is straightforward. The application timetable below will give you an idea of what you should be doing and when. Refer to the relevant chapters for further information.

(Note: this timetable doesn't apply only to A level students – it is for students doing any advanced or level 3 course.)

First year of A levels (fourth or fifth year in Scotland)

Autumn term

- Start to explore the range of possible options beyond your advanced-level courses at school or college (see Chapters 1 and 2).
- Consider your GCSE or equivalent qualifications – the range and grades achieved – and review any A level, Scottish Higher, International Baccalaureate (IB), Irish Leaving Certificate (ILC), Advanced

Diploma or BTEC National subjects that you are taking (see Chapter 6).

- Will your qualifications enable you to fulfil your future plans? Discuss this point with your careers adviser.

Spring term

- Work through a skills, aptitudes and interests guide, such as Centigrade or Morrisby, or complete a career development profiling exercise (see Chapter 2).
- Start to research your higher education options in the light of these results. Prepare for and attend a UCAS higher education convention (see Chapters 4 and 5).
- Explore the financial implications of attending a higher education course (see Chapter 3).

Summer term

- Prepare for and attend a UCAS convention, if you missed out on this in the spring (see Chapters 4 and 5).
- Continue to research your higher education options, checking UCAS course requirements and entry profiles.
- Draw up a shortlist of possible higher education institutions.
- Make decisions on courses and modules to take next year.
- Arrange to do work experience during the summer. This is an important prerequisite for entry to some courses, for example paramedical studies, medicine, veterinary science and veterinary medicine, social sciences, the land-based industries and teaching degree courses (see Chapter 2).
- Try to enlist sponsorship for courses – write to possible organisations you have researched (see Chapter 3).
- Start to organise your year out if you plan to take a gap year.
- Gather up material evidence from which to draft a personal statement for your UCAS application (see Chapter 17).

Summer holidays

- Undertake the work experience you arranged during the summer term. Keep a diary of what you did so that you can refer back to it when writing your personal statement (see Chapter 17).

Second year of A levels (fifth or sixth year in Scotland)

Autumn term

- Review your courses again now that your summer exam results are known.
- Before 20 September, consider whether to have your AS qualifications certificated. Get advice from your careers adviser or subject teacher if you are unsure.

- Between 1 September and 15 January – preferably as early as possible – submit your completed UCAS application using Apply (see Chapter 7 and Part III).
- Before 15 October, submit your UCAS application for the University of Oxford or Cambridge. If you are applying from outside the EU or you wish to be considered for an organ scholarship, you must submit a Cambridge Online Preliminary Application (COPA) form as well as a UCAS application. UK and other EU applicants do not need to do this. Applicants for the University of Oxford are not required to submit a separate application form but extra information is required for some international interviews and for choral or organ awards (see Chapter 8 and Part III).
- Before 15 October, submit all UCAS applications for entry to medicine, dentistry, veterinary science and veterinary medicine.

Spring term
- 15 January is the application deadline for UCAS to receive applications for all courses except those with a 15 October deadline and art and design courses with a 24 March deadline. Visit the UCAS course search tool at www.ucas.com to find out whether art and design courses have a 15 January or 24 March deadline.
- Apply for bursaries, sponsorship or scholarships as appropriate.
- Prepare for possible interviews with admissions tutors; role-play is useful here.
- Applicants from England, Wales and Northern Ireland should make their applications for financial assessment through the Student Loans Company, whatever your particular circumstances. Applicants from Scotland make their application for financial assessment to the Student Awards Agency for Scotland (SAAS).
- From 24 February, if you used all five choices in your application but are not holding an offer from a higher education institution, you can use the Extra option.
- 24 March is the application deadline for the receipt at UCAS of applications for art and design courses (except those listed with a 15 January deadline).
- By 31 March, universities and colleges are advised to send UCAS their decisions on all applications received by the 15 January deadline. (Their absolute deadline to inform UCAS of their decisions is 8 May.)

Summer term
- By 8 May decisions should have been received from all universities and colleges and you should have responded to any offers of places that you hold.
- Before 30 June, further applications can be made using UCAS Extra (if you applied for five courses originally and are not holding an offer). The end of June is the last date for receipt of all applications before Clearing.

Summer holidays

- 14 August is A level results day (Scottish Higher results come out in early August), when you may need additional support through UCAS Clearing to find an alternative higher education option or further information and guidance from your local careers service. Vacancy information is available from this date. If you have met all the conditions of your firm choice and exceeded at least one of these, you will be eligible to register to look for another course during the Adjustment period.
- 20 September is the last date for Clearing applications.

Part I
In the think tank

1 | Is higher education right for you?

Overview of higher education today

Applying for entry to higher education may well be the most important step that you've taken alone. There are plenty of individuals to consult to help you choose your higher education course and place of study – your careers adviser, your careers and subject teachers, your present employer, your parents (throughout this book, the term 'parents' should be read to mean parents or legal guardians), your partner and wider family and friends. But the decision is ultimately yours and, since it will affect your life for several years to come, you need to be confident about the suitability of your chosen higher education course.

Every year, people take up places only to find that the course content, teaching style or institution is not what they expected – and they subsequently drop out. The average drop-out rate, according to the Higher Education Statistics Agency, is 8.6%, but the rate at individual universities and colleges varies considerably. At one it is as low as 1.2%; at some, it is higher than 21.1%.

This can be difficult, not just for the student but also for the higher education institution, so it is worth taking the time at this stage to make sure that your application choices are really appropriate for you.

All about you

Before considering higher education courses, there are a few points on which you really need to know your own mind. Take a look at the questions in the following paragraphs and work out where you stand.

Are you happy to continue in education, full or part time, for a further two, three or four years?

Going on to higher education is a big step to take. Put simply, you've got to be committed and enthusiastic. If you do not enjoy your chosen studies, you will find your time in higher education very difficult.

Advanced-level study – for example GCE AS/A2, Scottish Higher, Irish Leaving Certificate (ILC), International Baccalaureate (IB), BTEC

National Award and so on – is essential preparatory learning for many aspects of higher education, not just in terms of subject-specific knowledge but also in terms of analytical skills. On your higher education course, you will be developing your powers of deduction, reasoning, critical analysis and evaluation just as much as you will be learning new facts about your chosen subject. Are you ready for this?

There are literally thousands of courses that are not straight developments of school- or college-based study – many are fascinating and worthwhile combinations that include opportunities for studying abroad. Does the thought of all this fill you with excitement or leave you pretty cold?

Do you have a strong and ongoing interest in self-development?

Your friends may already have started earning and could become more independent while you continue to study and accumulate sizeable debts. Can you be patient and philosophical, anticipating an interesting occupation and a better standard of living when you become an experienced graduate?

Do people around you (family, friends, girlfriend or boyfriend) appreciate and support your intention to continue your education? If they do not, do you anticipate that this will pose practical or emotional challenges for you? And if they do, will they be as understanding and continue to value and support you in two or three years' time?

Have you the mental strength to maintain self-belief and stick to your long-term aims if others withdraw their support?

Have you seriously explored your aptitudes, interests and career aspirations?

Do you want to learn more because you have strong ability in a particular area and because you find the subject matter interesting? If so, you are in a good starting position and are likely to enjoy your studies.

Some degree-level courses explore one particular subject area in great depth, with no obvious link to employment or a career structure (for example history, anthropology, geography, physics, English, American studies and French). Have you thought about what you will do once you graduate? How will your degree link with your long-term career plan? (See Chapter 2 for more on this.) A degree may only be a stepping stone to the start of a professional career – once you are in employment, it is often necessary to continue studying to gain professional qualifications. You will need commitment!

Some people are influenced by promotional publicity or by the enthusiasm of other people and do not consider the possible long-term impact of their choice on themselves. You need to think carefully about this.

Step back and try a number of aptitude and interest guides that are available online and in careers centres (see the 'Resources' section at the end of Chapter 2). You need to investigate the values and attitudes needed to strengthen your decision making.

Are you ready to be a student?

Student life is likely to offer you all of the social and extracurricular opportunities you ever dreamed of – are you confident that you will be able to balance your social life with your studies? Remember, there is a big change from the guided learning you have experienced at school or college to the self-management of study in higher education.

You will have to develop your own study skills and become an independent, self-motivated learner. Your subject teachers or tutors can offer helpful guidance on this point.

Do not be surprised if you feel confused and uncertain about applying to courses a long way from home. You are taking an important decision that may result in you striking out on your own, seemingly leaving behind everything you find familiar. It's natural to feel apprehensive about this – many people do experience insecurity and can feel isolated and disorientated at first, but most find they adapt very quickly.

If you are feeling very worried about the prospect of leaving home, talk to a friendly careers adviser, student adviser, personal tutor, or a friend or relative, and focus on the positive aspects of your higher education intentions. It is important to make sure you are clear about your plans and the changes these will mean for your day-to-day life.

Last – money. How you are going to finance your higher education course is likely to be a major consideration. This subject is discussed in depth in Chapter 3.

Conclusion

The decision to pursue a higher education course is not one that should be taken lightly. However, if you have read through the questions and points above and still feel confident that higher education is the right choice for you, read on. The rest of Part I will help you focus your research so that you can cut down the seemingly infinite number of courses on offer to the five you will enter on your UCAS application.

As you work through the following chapters, keep testing yourself by asking the following questions.

- Have I given enough consideration to this point?
- Which resources proved useful in my research?
- Have I talked to people with knowledge or experience in this area?
- Will I feel the same in two or three years' time?
- Should I do more research?

Essential research

- Talk to subject teachers, tutors or form teachers and careers advisers.
- Check to see whether your local careers or Connexions service gives information on higher education opportunities on its website.
- Use the timetable on pages 3 to 6 to draw up your own calendar of important dates and deadlines. Decisions about your aims and intentions need to be made by the end of September 2013, and all subsequent UCAS deadlines must then be met.

2| Looking to the future: career routes

Since you will be committing a lot of time and money to following a higher education course, it is vital to have researched possible career routes leading on from graduation. This is the moment for in-depth careers exploration and planning, looking at where a particular subject area might take you and also at what previous graduates have gone on to do.

This may seem very difficult. How can you possibly know yet what you want to do in four or more years' time? How can you ever narrow down the options when you are having enough trouble just choosing which courses to apply for? Some people, of course, do have firm career ideas. For others this idea of planning for the future can be difficult to face because it may seem that there is simply too much choice. It may also seem time consuming when you are busy working for exams.

It is good to have some career ideas though, not least because admissions tutors want to know that you are looking ahead, and that you are going to be an interested and motivated student with a career development plan that extends well beyond your time at university or college. If you are called to interview (see Chapter 9), having thought your plans through will mean you aren't floored by any career-related questions. An important thing to remember, however, is that any decisions you make or ideas you have at this stage are not set in stone. You can change and adapt your plans as you go along.

Developing a career plan

If you already have a career plan

If you already have a particular career in mind, now is the time to research it in as much depth as possible. Find out which courses are the most relevant, which get you professional accreditation in the career you have chosen (if applicable) and which have the best record of placing graduates in their chosen career area. For more on this, see Chapters 4 and 5.

If you already know what subject interests you, but you do not know what you want to do next

This is the time to do some broad research. Take a look at a careers directory or website (see the 'Resources' section at the end of this chapter) to find out what's out there, and focus on the jobs that seem to relate to your chosen subject. Research possible progression routes and projected salaries in different careers. You can also get ideas from the occupational destinations of graduates from major subject areas – this information is usually available on universities' and colleges' websites. Find out how many of last year's graduates are in full-time professional occupations drawing on their particular skills and abilities.

In addition to looking at universities' and colleges' own websites, you could consult the latest edition of *What Do Graduates Do?* by the Higher Education Careers Services Unit (HECSU), which gives the destinations of those who graduated in 2011 six months after graduation. Visit www.hecsu.ac.uk/current_projects_what_do_graduates_do.htm for more information.

Better still, try to find information on graduates' destinations one or two years on, if universities and colleges are able to provide this. They are required by the government to provide figures after six months, but this information is not particularly valuable because many graduates are in temporary employment at this stage while earning money to pay off debts or go travelling, or they are still in the process of applying for permanent jobs.

If you have no idea at all

If you're not sure what subject area interests you and you do not have a particular career in mind, it may be worth reconsidering whether higher education is really the right choice for you. On the other hand, if you are simply feeling bewildered by the number of options available to you, there are plenty of books, websites and ICT programs that can help you to assess your interests. Try a range of them, and take it from there.

> **TIP!**
>
> Remember – your careers adviser is always a good starting point.

The graduate skill set

Some courses lead naturally into a recognised career or occupational area (for example veterinary surgery, law, or hospitality and catering management), but most do not. For the majority of students, therefore, the value of higher education in terms of career prospects is that it enables you to develop a 'graduate skill set', because study of any subject at this level should develop your abilities in some of the areas regarded as important by employers, while other opportunities available in higher education can help you to develop other, equally valuable, skills.

What are these skills?

They are often known as non-technical, soft, transferable or employability skills. The report *Future fit: Preparing graduates for the world of work* produced by Universities UK and the Confederation of British Industry (CBI) was compiled from research conducted with major employers. In the introduction, the director-general of the CBI wrote:

> 'The recession – and the resulting increase in competition for jobs – throws into sharper focus the need for graduates to have the attributes to succeed in the workplace. In addition to acquiring the strong academic and technical knowledge required for many roles, our graduates and postgraduates also need the employability skills and positive attitude that employers value in every new recruit.'

The report concluded that employability skills were more important than the specific occupational, technical or academic knowledge or skills associated with the graduate's degree.

If you are interested, you can read this report at www.agcas.org.uk/agcas_resources/104-Future-fit-Preparing-graduates-for-the-world-of-work-.

So what are employability skills? They have different names in different organisations but they generally come under the following headings:

- business and customer awareness
- communication and literacy
- critical thinking
- entrepreneurship/enterprise
- IT
- managing complex information
- numeracy
- positive attitude
- problem solving
- research skills
- self-management
- team working.

Many degree and diploma programmes do not at first sight appear to develop such skills. But you could be surprised! If you check your chosen course at several different universities and colleges, using the

UCAS course search tool (more on this at the end of Chapter 4), and look under 'entry profiles' you will find the skills that they view as being provided by their degree programmes. The university careers advisory services may also be able to help. They are there to help students in all years, and making early contact can be very profitable.

Some universities and colleges include relevant modules in all their courses and issue students with a logbook or certificate that shows how they gained each skill. One, for instance, states that all its degree programmes include:

- analysis and solving problems
- team working and interpersonal skills
- verbal communication
- written communication
- personal planning and organising
- initiative
- numerical reasoning
- information literacy and ICT.

The above is not the case in all universities and colleges, but many careers services or employability centres now run separate employability and personal development courses on which you can enrol and that you follow at the same time as you work for your academic qualifications. These courses are well worth exploring when you arrive at university or college – and it's even more worthwhile if you sign up for them! You will normally receive an award that will be understood by many graduate employers who will be familiar with its content.

Many careers advisory services also run special sessions for students to help them understand which transferable skills are most in demand by employers and how to acquire them. Some workshops are run by major employers and include titles such as:

- commerciality – Ernst & Young
- commercial awareness – BDO LLP
- decision making for business – Deloitte
- how to develop your commercial instincts – Freshfields
- how to develop networking skills – Bloomberg
- presentation skills – Capita Consulting
- assessment centres – Capgemini
- interview skills – Logica
- preparing for psychometric assessment – PwC.

Having high-level skills in these areas will increase your appeal to prospective employers, which is essential in the present climate. With severe competition for the best graduate jobs, employers are able to pick and choose. You might like to see what is offered in the way of employability skills training before you make your final choice of course and university or college.

However, as stated earlier, some university and college admissions tutors – and some graduate employers – will also require you to have demonstrated your interest in your chosen career area through work experience or work placements *before you apply for a higher education place through UCAS*. This is a major reason why it is important to think hard about your career aspirations as early as possible.

Work experience

Now

Being able to write about suitable work experience on your UCAS form will, for many courses, boost your application. Many courses (those linked with health or social care and with careers in the land-based industries, for example) nearly always expect applicants to have arranged some experience – even for a short period – in a relevant job. Maybe your school or college is already on to this and has arranged some form of work experience or shadowing for you. If not, you could try to arrange something yourself to take place in the holidays.

It isn't always possible, however. Some professionals, such as doctors, vets, accountants and lawyers, are often flooded with requests from students. In addition they have the problem of contacting patients or clients to ask if they will agree to have a student present.

If you cannot get any experience in the profession you are hoping to enter, there are alternatives. You could, for example, visit law courts and observe different kinds of trial. If you cannot arrange work experience in a hospital or with a GP, you could try to observe what goes on at a typical doctor's practice. You could ask if it is possible to spend some time with the practice nurse or healthcare assistant.

If you cannot find any opportunities in a relevant profession, you could still demonstrate that you have the right sort of personal skills by doing paid or voluntary work in a caring environment where you will learn to work with people directly, for example in a children's nursery or a day centre for people with disabilities, or with a volunteer agency such as a drug rehabilitation centre or a night shelter for homeless people.

If you have a part-time job in a supermarket you could ask to talk to the manager and find out what it is like managing people in a business environment.

> **TIP!**
>
> Admissions tutors are impressed by applicants who have built up knowledge of a related work sector and whose plans include developing useful employment links while studying.
>
> If you have really tried hard to obtain work experience but have been unsuccessful, explain this on your UCAS application and describe the related activities that you have undertaken as an alternative.

While in higher education

The same points apply once you get to university or college. You will probably need to work during term time, so look first for relevant experience. Try to spend time in a job that will broaden your experience and give you insight into a potential employment area. If that is not possible, do your best to draw up a list of soft skills applicable to any career that you have acquired from experience in any kind of job – bar work, sales . . . whatever you can find.

Your university's careers advisory service or student services unit can usually help and may run a job shop especially to find part-time opportunities for students. They can also provide details of vacation work placements – and may even be able to give you a grant to help with additional expenses you might incur on a placement.

Conclusion

It's helpful to have a career path in mind, even if it might change later as you progress through your course and gain experience. The earlier you start your research, the better your chance of making an informed decision – with the added benefit that evidence of your long-term approach will strengthen your UCAS application and improve your interview performance.

Resources

Publications

- *Choosing Your Degree Course & University*, Trotman, www.trotman.co.uk.
- *Getting into* series, Trotman, www.trotman.co.uk. Gives advice on securing a place at university for courses leading to professional careers (such as medicine, law, psychology, physiotherapy, engineering, veterinary school, and business, economics and manage-

ment courses), and on gaining places on courses at Oxford and Cambridge.

- *The Graduate Jobs Formula*, Trotman, www.trotman.co.uk. A guide to securing a job after graduation, whatever your degree.
- *How to Write a Winning UCAS Personal Statement*, Trotman, www.trotman.co.uk.
- *If Only I'd Known*, Association of Graduate Recruiters, www.agr.org.uk/write/Documents/Reports/If_Only_I'd_Known.pdf. Contains tips on making the most of university and how to gain the skills that graduate employers are looking for.
- *The UCAS Guide to Getting into University and College*, UCAS, www.ucasbooks.com.
- *What Do Graduates Do?*, HECSU and Association of Graduate Careers Advisory Services (AGCAS), www.hecsu.ac.uk.

ICT programs

- Careerscape: information on careers and higher education courses, together with case studies and articles. This may be available in your school or college, at your local careers service or library (CASCAiD, www.cascaid.co.uk).
- Centigrade (endorsed by UCAS): gauges your academic and personal strengths (Cambridge Occupational Analysts, www.coa.co.uk).
- Job Explorer Database (Jed): interactive, multimedia careers information resource in which students can explore over 800 jobs in depth (2,200 individual career titles), with pictures and case studies of people at work. The section 'Higher ideas' shows which higher education courses connect with interests and subject choices (Careersoft, www.careersoft.co.uk).
- eCLIPS: allows users to search for careers against criteria such as work skills or school subjects, and also has a linked interest guide. This may be available in your school or college, at your local careers service or library (www.eclips-online.co.uk).

Websites

- www.agcas.org.uk: Association of Graduate Careers Advisory Services.
- www.careersa-z.co.uk: alphabetical listing of careers with links to many other websites.
- www.gov.uk: this site is useful if you are considering whether higher education is right for you (click on 'Education and learning').
- www.prospects.ac.uk: useful detailed information on graduate careers.

3 | A matter of money

If you have got this far in the book, you are serious about putting in a higher education application. Even before considering whether you are likely to achieve the entry grades for the course, you will probably have asked yourself 'Can I afford it?'

Certainly, you will need to think through your finances very carefully and research all the types of assistance that will be available to you. There is a lot of information available – on government websites, on the UCAS website, from universities and colleges themselves and in books written specifically on this subject. A summary is given in this chapter, with details of where to look for more information in the 'Resources' section at the end.

In order to help you in your overall consideration of whether higher education is right for you, this chapter will look at the two main costs in attending higher education: tuition fees and living expenses.

Tuition fees

The cost of providing college and university courses is met partly by the government and partly through variable (top-up) tuition fees, which are the student's contribution.

The maximum annual tuition fees for students in England, Northern Ireland and Wales are £9,000. All universities and colleges are allowed to charge up to £6,000; if they wish to charge higher fees up to £9,000 they must prove that they are awarding bursaries to poorer students. Universities and colleges decide for themselves how much to charge. The majority charge the full £9,000 for all or some of their courses, but others have opted for lower amounts – some as low as £4,000. There is no national list of fees charged – you will have to check individual websites.

You will not have to pay these fees in advance, however, unless you are able and willing to do so. You may take out a tuition fee loan; this is not means-tested and will not have to be repaid until after graduation when you are in employment and your earnings have reached £21,000. This amount is standard, but there are variations in how the rules are applied by individual nations within the UK.

The situation for students resident in one part of the UK but studying in another is complicated. Northern Irish, Scottish and Welsh universities will charge non-resident students higher tuition fees than those charged to their own residents. A summary of the information known at the time of writing (April 2013) follows. However, please check national websites for more recent information.

- In England, tuition fees are up to £9,000. The average in 2013 was £8,389. When bursaries and tuition waivers were taken into account the average became £7,898.
- In Northern Ireland, tuition fees for Northern Ireland residents are capped at £3,635 and will rise only in line with inflation until at least 2015. (In 2013–2014 for example, they were £3,575.) Fees for other UK students attending university in Northern Ireland are not capped and could be up to £9,000.
- In Wales, tuition fees are up to £9,000 a year, but Welsh students pay a lower rate of £3,465 – this also applies if they study elsewhere in the UK. The difference is made up by the Welsh Assembly Government, which awards non-means-tested tuition fee grants to cover the difference between the maximum tuition fee loan (see page 24 for a definition) and the actual figure charged by some universities and colleges.
- In Scotland, Scottish students studying at Scottish universities pay no fees. Students from England, Wales and Northern Ireland studying in Scotland must pay the full fees charged by individual universities and colleges. (These are lower than in England, with an average of approximately £6,840.)

Living expenses

These cover the cost of your accommodation, food, clothes, travel and books and equipment (plus possible extras such as field trips and study visits, if these are not covered by the tuition fees), as well as leisure and social activities.

It is very difficult to find out what these living expenses might be! All the official websites are very helpful in telling you what financial assistance will be available, but they do not tell you what you will need to budget for. (This is obviously difficult since individual students' tastes, needs and priorities vary widely.) The information below gives you some idea of possible expenses.

- Try individual universities' and colleges' websites. Some are better than others and give breakdowns under various headings such as accommodation, food and daily travel. Others go further and give typical weekly, monthly or annual spends. If they appear to give no information, try looking under 'International students'. Most universities and colleges are keen to attract international students and therefore publish suggested figures for their living costs. They don't give this information in a standard format. Some give weekly figures; some monthly; others for an academic year. You need to know how many weeks this means before you can compare like with like – and if you are reading information for international students you also need to be sure that it does not include any vacation weeks. (Their suggested budgets are often given for term time plus Christmas and Easter vacations, which they may spend in the UK.) Inexplicably, the figures are often at least one year out of date – which seems strange, given their importance to potential students.

- A quick snapshot shows that for autumn 2013 a university in a Midlands English city suggested £307 a week; one in London £284 per week; one on the south coast between £814 and £1,150 per month; one in the South West of England £8,100 for the academic year (including *all* meals); while one in Scotland suggested £695 a month. Costs always vary according to whether students live in university-owned or private accommodation.
- If you look at www.natwest.com you can consult the Student Living Index, which was last compiled in 2010 from a survey using a sample of 2,500 students in 25 university towns and cities. Costs are analysed for average local weekly student expenditure on living and accommodation (books and course materials, clothes, entertainment and eating out, food, laundry, rent, transport costs, telephone bills, utility bills, alcohol, cigarettes, CDs, DVDs, photocopying and library costs). The cost of living at each of these universities is then compared.
- The NUS (nus.org.uk) gives average costs in towns throughout the UK, but their survey refers to England only.
- A survey, *Student Income and Expenditure Study 2012*, by the National Centre for Social Research (NatCen) in partnership with the Institute for Employment Studies, was commissioned by the Department for Business, Innovation and Skills. Over 4,000 students at almost 100 universities and colleges across England and Wales were expected to take part in the study. Results should be available at natcen.ac.uk sometime in 2013.

You will probably be surprised when you consult some of these sources to find that the cheapest and most expensive towns are not as you expected. Much depends on how much accommodation the university or college owns (as opposed to having students living in often more expensive privately rented houses and flats) and how much daily travel costs come to.

Funding your studies

How do you intend to fund your time in higher education? Don't ignore this question and leave it until the last minute! You will need to think carefully about how to budget for several years' costs – and you need to know what help you might be able to expect from:

- the government
- your parents or partner
- other sources.

This chapter gives a brief overview of a very complicated funding situation, which varies according to where you come from and where you plan to study. For more detail about all the different types of funding available and how to apply for them, please consult your own national website.

All figures quoted here applied to students beginning their courses in 2013 (figures for the academic year beginning in 2014 were not available at the time of publication).

Tuition fee loans

These are available in England, Northern Ireland and Wales. If you take one out (and most students do), the Student Loans Company will pay your fees directly to your university or college at the start of each year of your course, adding the interest to your repayable loan total. The loan will be repaid through the income tax system. That means that once you are working, your employer will take the required amount from your salary and make the payments – 9% of your income above that £21,000 level. Payments increase when graduates earn above £41,000. (If you had started repaying the loan, then lost your job or had a pay cut, then your repayments would drop accordingly.)

- The £21,000 threshold is designed to rise in line with average earnings from April 2017.
- The interest rate for students starting their courses in 2013 was 6.6% (based on the retail prices index (RPI) plus 3%).
- If you have not cleared your debt 30 years after graduation, it will be cancelled.
- At the time of writing the Welsh Assembly had announced that it would cancel up to £1,500 from students' loan repayments as soon as they began to repay their loans.

Maintenance or living costs loans

In addition to a tuition fee loan, all students may apply for a maintenance or living cost loan. The maximum amount is £7,675, but not all students are entitled to this sum. Everyone may have 65% of it but the remaining 35% will depend on your and your family's income – in other words, it is means-tested. 'Family income' means a household's – student's, parent's or partner's – residual income, or their income before tax and after any pensions contributions and allowances for dependent children have been deducted.

For students starting their courses in 2013, the maximum annual loan in England was:

- £4,375 for those living in the family home
- £5,500 for those studying away from home (£7,675 in London)
- £6,535 for students spending a year of a UK course overseas.

In Northern Ireland:

- £3,750 for those living in the family home
- £4,840 for those studying away from home (£6,780 in London)
- £5,770 for students spending a year of a UK course overseas.

In Scotland:

- £5,500 whether living at home or elsewhere.

And in Wales, the figures were:

- £3,987 for those living in the family home
- £5,150 for those studying away from home (£7,215 in London)
- £6,140 for students spending a year of a UK course overseas.

These loans are repaid in the same way as loans for tuition fees.

Maintenance grants

In England, non-repayable grants of up to £3,354 a year are available to students whose household income is less than £42,611. They are means-tested, so the maximum amount is only available if your household's annual income is below £25,000. However, if you get a grant your maintenance loan may be reduced.

In Northern Ireland, the maximum maintenance grant to resident students is £3,475 with an upper income limit of £41,065.

In Wales, for resident students the Maintenance Grant is replaced by the Assembly Learning Grant, worth up to £5,161 a year and payable to students whose family income is below £50,020.

In Scotland, the grant is replaced by a Young Students' Bursary of up to £1,750.

Bursaries

In addition to the funding described above, most universities and colleges offer tuition fee bursaries, mainly to students who receive the maximum maintenance loan. These bursaries cover part or all of the cost of the course and are awarded according to the universities' own criteria, but they are often worked out according to the level of parental income or maintenance grant that you receive.

Additional support

Additional financial support is available to students with disabilities and for students with dependants – for example, those whose partner is also a student, provided that one or both are responsible for a young person in full-time education below higher education level. These regulations are subject to change so it is essential to check them.

Other forms of support are available in different parts of the UK. For example, English universities may offer scholarships under the National Scholarship Programme (NSP), which gives financial help to students resident in and studying in England, whose tuition fees are over £6,000 and whose family income is £25,000 or less, usually in the form of a fee waiver of up to £3,000, or one of the following: subsidised accommodation, a cash bursary of up to £1,000, or some other form of help.

Awards are paid by universities and colleges. Each university or college has its own rules about eligibility and what types of award are available. You can find a list of universities and colleges participating in the scheme at www.hefce.ac.uk/whatwedo/wp/currentworktowidenparticipation/ nationalscholarshipprogramme. If a university or college is not listed, it does not take part in the programme. NSP scholarships are awarded in addition to any other loans or grants students might apply for.

Welsh National Bursaries of at least £347 may be available to residents of Wales who are paying the full tuition fee amount and receive the full amount of Assembly Learning Grant.

Other bursaries and scholarships

Students on particular courses, with particular career aspirations or with particular personal circumstances may be eligible for extra financial help. It is worth consulting the sources listed at the end of this chapter to find out whether you might be eligible for a grant made by a particular professional organisation or charity.

Sponsorship

Students applying for particular courses – for example accountancy, business studies and engineering – can sometimes be sponsored by employers or related organisations. In return for a sum of money paid to you as a student you would normally be expected to work for your sponsor during some of your vacations. Naturally, if you were suitable they would expect you to work for them for a period after you graduated.

NHS Bursaries

Students on nursing and certain healthcare* courses are eligible for additional funding from the NHS. Amounts vary according to the course and according to where students live. The package includes:

- free tuition
- a non-means-tested grant
- a means-tested bursary
- a reduced-rate non-means-tested loan.

> **TIP!**
>
> Make a note of any deadlines for loan or funding applications and ensure that you have completed all of the necessary paperwork.

Other sources of cash

Part-time work

For many students, there will be a continual need to balance studies with part-time employment. And this is something to think about when you make your selection of universities and colleges. Some towns have many, many more opportunities than others. In an area of high unemployment, for instance, all the jobs may be taken by permanent workers. In more affluent areas there might be more hourly paid work available – especially at hours when students are willing to work. You can check out the local employment situation on universities' and colleges' websites.

Here are some additional ideas to bear in mind.

- Many universities and colleges help by running their own jobs banks. Students can get work, for example, in the students' union, libraries or offices (secretarial and clerical work if they have the skills), or in catering, domestic or manual work.
- Other opportunities often include guiding visitors around the campus or acting as student guides on open days.

* The above does not refer to student doctors and dentists, who are treated in the same way as students on all degree programmes for the first four years of their degree courses. NHS funding is available to them from the fifth year.

- Most universities and colleges also have a job shop provided by student services or the careers advisory service that advertises jobs in the town or city.
- A useful website with a number of part-time jobs is www.hotrecruit. com.
- Another, with a particularly creative approach to the issue, is www. slivers.com. This service is not available everywhere but where it does run it matches your sliver of time – e.g. 'three hours next Tuesday' – with a suitable local employer's requirements.

However, many higher education courses include practical coursework, field studies and/or time spent abroad, which leave little opportunity for employment except during vacations. Additionally, it is often recommended that students spend no more than 15 hours a week in paid employment if their studies are not to suffer. Oxford and Cambridge do not encourage any of their students to work during their (particularly short) term times.

> **TIP!**
>
> Check the cost of living and employment availability in the towns where you might be going to live during term time. This will help you estimate what your living costs are likely to be and your chances of finding part-time work.

Banking deals

Many students take advantage of the student banking deals available from a number of high street banks. These can include interest-free overdrafts (which are advisable as a last resort only because they do have to be repaid – and interest rates on late payments can be very high) as well as various other freebies such as free driving lessons or railcards. You should shop around carefully for the deal that best suits your priorities – and remember, the advice that banks give on their websites is unlikely to be wholly impartial.

> **TIP!**
>
> Try not to run up a big bank overdraft or credit card debts, as in the long run you can end up paying large sums of interest on the money owed.

Many universities and colleges have student financial advisers whom students can approach for help. A students' union is also a good source of information and advice on financial assistance.

Students from the European Union

Students from the rest of the European Union pay the same tuition fees as UK students and may be eligible to apply for a tuition fees loan (or free tuition in Scotland). You should apply to the appropriate authority – Student Finance England, Student Finance Northern Ireland, Student Finance Wales or the SAAS as appropriate (see the 'Resources' section at the end of this chapter for the various websites).

TIP!

All students are advised to apply to the appropriate authority for funding as soon as they have firmly accepted an offer of a place.

Conclusion

Money can be a major headache for students, so it is well worth taking the time to work out how you're going to fund yourself. It's also very important to be on top of all the paperwork required for loan applications because missed deadlines can mean that you start your course before your loan comes through.

Resources

Publications

- Various Child Poverty Action Group titles, for example *Welfare Benefits and Tax Credits Handbook*, *Council Tax Handbook* and *Child Support Handbook*, for England, Wales and Northern Ireland. Available at www.cpag.org.uk.
- For Scottish residents, as above plus *Benefits for Students in Scotland Handbook*, available from Child Poverty Action Group in Scotland at www.cpag.org.uk/scotland.
- *Cut the Cost of Uni*, Trotman, www.trotman.co.uk.

Official organisations

- www.gov.uk: contains a student finance calculator (www.gov.uk/student-finance-calculator).
- www.studentfinanceengland.co.uk.
- www.studentfinanceni.co.uk.
- www.studentfinancewales.co.uk.
- www.saas.gov.uk.

- www.gov.uk/extra-money-pay-university (for information on bursaries and scholarships).

General student support

- www.everythingyouwantedtoknow.com: links to sources of information on funding and sponsorships.
- www.moneysavingexpert.com/students: site of money expert Martin Lewis, which gives helpful advice on all aspects of student budgeting.
- www.nhsbsa.nhs.uk/816.aspx: information on NHS student bursaries.
- www.nus.org.uk: the National Union of Students site.
- www.ucas.com/students/studentfinance.
- www.slc.co.uk: the Student Loans Company.
- www.family-action.org.uk/section.aspx?id=1037: Educational Grants Advisory Service (EGAS), which is primarily concerned with helping disadvantaged students.

Part-time and temporary jobs

- www.student-jobs.co.uk.
- www.justjobs4students.com.

4| Choosing what to study

You are probably already aware that there is a vast number of subjects on offer. You can get an idea of the full range by exploring the UCAS search tool at www.ucas.com and the other resources listed on page 37.

You may enter up to five course choices on your UCAS application. However, if you are applying for medicine, dentistry or veterinary science you are limited to four courses in your chosen subject, although you can make one additional application to a course in another subject – see Chapter 8 for more information.

So how do you start to narrow it down? This chapter covers some of the questions you should be asking yourself so that you can focus your research on the courses that will be best suited to your interests.

Which subject area?

If you have got this far, it is likely that you have some idea of what subject area you would like to pursue further. If not, here are a few questions to think about.

- Which of the subjects you are currently studying interests you most? Are you interested enough to want to study it for the next few years?
- Are you interested in one particular aspect of your advanced-level course? If so, you may find that specialist higher education courses will allow you to focus on this particular aspect.
- What are your career aspirations? What are the entry requirements for that career? Which courses match this best?
- Are you prepared to undergo more specific job-related training as a postgraduate? If not, should you be looking for a vocational course that leads directly into an occupation?

You could try using Centigrade (www.coa2.co.uk/centigrade) to indicate courses that might appeal to you. You do this by completing an online questionnaire which is used to assess your interests, abilities and personal qualities. This assessment matches your replies with courses of higher education at mainly degree, HND or Diploma levels. You will receive a list of courses to investigate and an action plan suggesting further research. The cost is £15 for an email report or £25 for a printed version (£30 if outside the UK to cover postage). The 'Resources' section at the end of Chapter 2 should give you some more ideas of where to start your research.

Which qualification?

It is important to know something about each of the different types of qualification on offer so that you can select the one that is most suitable for you.

For example, course lengths (and therefore expense) vary widely. A list of the main options is given below, and each course type is explored in more depth in the paragraphs that follow.

- DipHEs
- HNDs
- foundation degrees
- ordinary first degrees: the lowest grade of degree awarded
- honours first degrees: divided into four classes (first, upper second, lower second and third)
- courses leading to the award of a master's degree.

See the 'Degree courses' section below for further explanation of first (or bachelor's) degrees and master's degrees.

DipHEs

Some universities and colleges offer undergraduate diplomas leading to a DipHE (Diploma of Higher Education). Two-year full-time DipHE courses are normally equivalent to the first two years of a degree and can often be used for entry to the final year of a related degree course. They are mainly linked to vocational areas such as health and social care, paramedic practice and youth work, although some universities and colleges offer them in other subject areas such as business studies.

HNDs

Many universities and colleges offer two-year BTEC or Scottish Qualifications Authority (SQA) HND courses. These are often offered in the same subject areas as the university's or college's degree courses, giving students the option to transfer between courses or to top up their HND to a degree through a further year's study. Keep this in mind when planning your application strategy. With a few exceptions such as health and social care, performing arts and hospitality management, HNDs fall into two main subject areas: science and engineering, and business studies and related subjects.

Science and engineering

Science and engineering courses at all levels attract comparatively fewer applications than business and finance courses. It is therefore likely that if you apply for a degree in, for example, mechanical engineering at an institution that also offers an HND in engineering, admissions tutors will make you an offer covering both the degree and the HND course, but with different conditions for each (normally lower for the HND). If you can achieve the minimum entry qualifications for a degree course, you should aim for these grades in subject areas such as science and engineering, unless you positively want to take a more vocational HND course (which many students do).

Business studies and related subjects

For HND courses in this subject area, the picture is rather different. HND courses usually attract a large number of applications in their own right: many students deliberately opt for the HND courses because they are shorter and often more specialised than the degrees. It is therefore very unusual for universities and colleges to make dual offers for degrees and HNDs. This means that you must consider your options very carefully.

If you have doubts about your ability to reach the level required for degree entry, you may be best advised to apply for the HND. You must talk through the options with your teachers or careers adviser before making these difficult decisions.

Foundation degrees

These courses are mainly offered in colleges of further or higher education in partnership with universities. Full-time courses last two years and, like HNDs, can be converted into honours degrees with a subsequent year of full-time study. Designed by business and industry to meet their skills needs, foundation degrees were originally developed to train employees in particular career sectors as higher technicians or associate professionals, but entry to full-time courses is now available to anyone.

Foundation degrees combine academic study with the development of work-related skills. Like HNDs (which in some subject areas they have replaced), they are often offered in the same subject areas as the university's degree courses, giving students the option to transfer between courses and to top up their foundation degree to an honours degree through a further year's study. Programmes are offered in areas such as digital media arts, business and management, horticulture, equine studies, hospitality, fashion design and a vast range of other subjects. Foundation degree courses lead to the awards of:

- FdA (arts)
- FdEng (engineering)
- FdSci (science).

In 2012, 21,525 applicants were accepted onto foundation degree programmes, a 16.4% decrease on the previous year (source: UCAS End of Cycle, December 2012). All potential full-time foundation degree students use Apply for entry to courses; part-time applicants make a direct application to individual colleges.

Degree courses

Bachelor's degrees

In England, Northern Ireland and Wales, first degree courses usually last three years (sometimes four, if a year abroad or in industry is included) and lead to the award of a bachelor's degree. The title of the degree awarded usually reflects the subject studied.

Some of the more common ones are:

- BA: Bachelor of Arts
- BCom: Bachelor of Commerce
- BEng: Bachelor of Engineering
- BMus: Bachelor of Music
- BSc: Bachelor of Science
- LLB: Bachelor of Law.

The exceptions to this are the universities of Oxford and Cambridge (Oxbridge), which award a BA regardless of the subject. (Oxbridge graduates are then able to upgrade to a master's degree, without further exams, about four years later.)

Master's degrees

In England, Northern Ireland and Wales, master's degrees are usually acquired via a completely different course that must be applied for separately and cannot be taken until the bachelor's degree has been completed.

However, some first degree courses lead directly to the award of a master's degree (e.g. MEd, MEng, MPhys and MSc). These courses are usually extended or enhanced versions of the bachelor's course, last at least four years, and are likely to be in engineering or science disciplines.

Scottish universities

At Scottish universities all standard bachelor's degrees last for four years rather than three. At some universities students are awarded a master's as standard for a four-year degree in arts, humanities and social science subjects while science students receive a BSc. Most students in Scotland enter university aged 18 after six years of secondary education, although a significant minority will enter after only five years and therefore be 17 when they start university.

Single, joint or combined honours?

Most universities and colleges offer single, joint and combined honours degree courses. Combined honours courses enable you to combine several areas of interest and may lead you to an interesting programme or additional career opportunities (for example, studying biology with French may enable you to work in France).

However, if you intend to take a joint or combined honours course, do be aware that you will be kept busier than you would be on a single honours course. It can be a struggle if you have to make your own connections between the modules of study, and the work may not be well coordinated. Question individual departments' admissions tutors as soon as possible about the possibilities and potential problems of combining courses.

Degree classification

Honours degrees are classified as:

- First Class
- Upper Second Class (2.i)
- Lower Second Class (2.ii)
- Third Class.

Ordinary and pass degrees are awarded, depending on the system, to those not pursuing honours courses or to narrow failures on honours courses.

Which mode of study?

Many degrees and HNDs can be studied as sandwich courses. These come in two varieties.

1. **Thick sandwich courses:** these include a full year spent on an industrial, commercial or professional training placement.
2. **Thin sandwich courses:** these include several sessions of a few weeks' work experience spread throughout the course.

Sponsorship is sometimes tied in with sandwich courses. Normally, you apply for a sandwich degree or HND course through UCAS and your university or college arranges your training placement.

However, if a sponsor requires you to attend a particular university or college, the sponsor will inform you and the institution will sort out the UCAS arrangements.

You may also be able to choose between full-time and part-time courses – the latter are becoming more popular as students increasingly find it necessary to work in order to finance their studies; on the other hand, it can be difficult to balance the demands of a job and higher education, so you should make sure you do some thorough research.

Which courses?

This is, of course, the million-dollar question! Having thought about the above points, you should now have a clearer idea of the type of qualification and subject area for which you would like to apply. However, there may still be hundreds of courses on offer fitting the criteria you have determined so far – so this is the point where you really must start to narrow down your options. The only way to do this is by thorough research, which means looking through directories, prospectuses and websites and visiting specific departments at specific universities.

Here are some of the things you should take into account.

- **Course content:** there can be a whole world of difference between courses with exactly the same title, so take a detailed look at the content and see how it relates to your particular interests. How much do you want to specialise? How much freedom do you want to select your options?
- **Teaching and assessment methods:** again, these can vary widely. For example, some courses may be very practical, with workshops and case studies, while others may be centred on essays and tutorials. If you do not perform well in exams, you can search for courses assessed via modules and projects.
- **Professional accreditation:** if you are planning to enter a specific career for which professional accreditation is required (for example law, engineering or accountancy), it is well worth checking out which courses offer full or partial exemption from the exams required to gain this accreditation.
- **Links with industry:** some courses and departments have strong links with industry, which can help graduates secure jobs.
- **Graduate destinations:** these are often listed on universities' and colleges' websites and can help you assess whether the course will give you the skills you will need in the workplace.

> **TIP!**
>
> Use the UCAS course search tool, which enables you to search courses by a wide range of features including subject, qualification, region and campus. There is also the ability to filter searches by fees, professional bodies, entry year and single or combined subjects. You will also find entry requirements for courses and access to university and college websites.

Conclusion

Based on these factors, you should be able to begin to develop a clear idea of the kind of course you would like to apply for. However, two aspects of the decision-making process have yet to be discussed: your choice of university or college and entry requirements. These factors are examined in detail in the following chapters.

Resources

Publications

- *Choosing Your Degree Course & University*, Trotman, www.trotman.co.uk.
- *Heap 2014: University Degree Course Offers*, Trotman, www.trotman.co.uk.
- *Progression* series, UCAS, www.ucasbooks.com.
- *The UCAS Guide to Getting into University and College*, UCAS, www.ucasbooks.com.
- *What Do Graduates Do?*, HECSU and AGCAS, www.hecsu.ac.uk.

ICT programs

- Higher Ideas: generates suggested higher education courses based on current studies, interests and career ambitions. This may be available at your school, college or local careers centre (www.careersoft.co.uk/Products/Higher_Ideas).

Websites

- www.ucas.com/students: see the UCAS course search tool and Apply.
- www.coa2.co.uk/centigrade: Centigrade.
- www.hefce.ac.uk: Higher Education Funding Council for England.

5 | Choosing where to study

The previous chapter should have helped you build up a picture of your ideal course and start to create a shortlist. However, it's still likely that a lot more than five courses will fit the bill, so you need to narrow the list down further.

Now is the time to start thinking about which institution you would like to study at.

Working out your priorities

There are over 300 institutions in the UCAS scheme that offer higher education courses, including universities, colleges of higher education and further education colleges. Very different considerations and priorities affect each person's choice of institution. To give you some idea of the range, current students say they were influenced by one or more of the following factors.

- Location: do you prefer an urban or a rural setting? Do you want to be on a campus or in the middle of a city? Are you trying to stay within easy reach of home, or get as far away as possible?
- Size of university.
- Popularity of university.
- Facilities for sport, leisure activities, music, etc.
- Accommodation: is there enough of it? Does it suit your preferences, e.g. self-catering or with meals provided?
- Famous alumni.
- Price of beer.
- Male to female ratio(!).

On a more serious note, they also mention these influences.

- Reputation for research or specialism in a particular department.
- Quality of course teaching.
- Status of university as a whole, which can be a perplexing concept: if you feel concerned about this point, you will need to seek advice from professional bodies and/or large employers.
- Employability of a particular institution's graduates.

- Number of student places on particular courses: the bigger the intake target, usually the better your chances. Prospectuses and websites give an indication of the size of intake, but remember that their numbers may include students on both single and combined or modular degrees.
- Entry requirements: be honest with yourself about your prospects at advanced level. It is better to face reality now than to be forced to revise your plans several months later.
- Cost of living.
- Financial support offered to students (e.g. bursaries and scholarships).
- Level of support and facilities for students with disabilities.

The list of factors you might want to consider could go on forever. You will have to draw the line somewhere and then work out which are most important to you personally.

Once you have decided on your key priorities, where do you start to find out the answers to all your questions? The 'Resources' section at the end of this chapter lists publications that collate this type of information. Using these as a first port of call can speed up your research no end, but there is no substitute for first-hand research through, for example, university open days, websites and prospectuses.

It is also well worth talking to former students from your school or college, family friends and older brothers and sisters about their experiences. More advice on this is given in the 'Researching your shortlist' section below.

> **TIP!**
>
> Do not forget to get university prospectuses and look at universities' websites.

Staying close to home?

A growing number of students apply only to universities and colleges that are within daily commuting distance, opting to save on living expenses while enjoying the support and comforts of home. With tuition fees of up to £9,000 for 2014 entry (depending on which country in the UK you live in and where in the UK you choose to study), the choice of living in a hall of residence or in rented accommodation may be an option for fewer and fewer students. But, don't forget, as mentioned in Chapter 3, in some towns where you might assume that living costs are high, rents can be lower than you think and it can be very easy to find part-time jobs.

Studying from home can limit your 'student experience', as time spent travelling cuts down your opportunities for involvement in societies and social activities. You may also be less likely to network and make new friends, especially if you still have close friends from school living in the area. For parents and siblings, having a full-time student living at home can create tensions as time goes by.

You may decide on a compromise solution. A growing number of higher education courses – HNDs, foundation degrees, even first degree courses – start with a year studying at a local, franchised further education college before transferring to the parent campus to complete your degree.

Researching your shortlist

As soon as you feel ready, draw up your shortlist of about 10 possible courses from which you will select up to five (or four) final choices for your UCAS application. For each of your shortlist entries, make sure you have considered the following questions.

- What will I actually be studying on this course?
- Do I like the environment?
- Where will I live?
- Which options can I select on this course?
- How is progress assessed?
- Is there a tutorial system and how much support and advice on learning do students get?
- Can I achieve the qualifications needed for entry? (For help on this last point, see the next chapter.)

Attend open days and taster sessions at universities and colleges that really appeal to you, and talk with student ambassadors, who will attempt to answer your questions on any subject. You can also write and arrange a visit to the department by yourself. Also make sure to spend some time in the town or city where the college or university is based; it is really important that you have some experience of a place where you may spend three or four years.

> **TIP!**
>
> Keep the prospectuses of places to which you are definitely applying!

For students with disabilities, this is particularly important – you need to make sure before you apply to an institution that it will be able to meet your particular needs. For example, some campuses are better than others for wheelchairs, while some have special facilities for people who are visually impaired or deaf. Get in touch with the disability officers at your shortlisted universities or colleges. More information about access and facilities for students with disabilities is also available at www.ucas.com and, of course, from the prospectuses and websites of the universities and colleges themselves.

Parents can help with weighing up the issues and are excellent as sounding boards, but their advice and knowledge on today's degree courses, their applicability and relevance may well be out of date. (For example, some of the new UK universities have the best resourced and most reputable courses of applied study that feed into new careers in multimedia and technological industries – but, equally, some of the newer universities and colleges are under-resourced and have poor teaching reputations.)

If you feel at all unsure about your choice of subject, enquire at each of your shortlisted universities and colleges to find out whether it is pos-sible to transfer from one course to another once your course has started.

Many universities and colleges supply entry details for their courses – accessible on the UCAS website – which can help with the decision-making process. You should also attend your nearest UCAS higher education convention to talk directly with representatives from higher education about courses.

Read the details concerning courses that interest you and for which you think realistically that you can match the entry requirements. Highlight important points you may want to address in the personal statement part of your UCAS application, or refer to at interview, several months ahead.

> **TIP!**
>
> Do not take anything as given. Email or phone departments directly and ask to speak to the admissions tutor if you want to ask ques-tions about the destinations of course graduates, possible career progression, admission details – anything. Tutors can be helpful and informative: they aren't there just to teach.

Selecting the final five

If there is one particular university or college you want to attend (perhaps because you are a mature student and cannot move away from home), you can use your choices to apply for more than one course at the same institution. (Note that this is not possible at

Oxbridge.) On the other hand, at some universities or colleges it is not necessary to apply for more than one course because admission is to a faculty or group of related subjects.

The other major factor to consider in selecting your final five courses is the entry requirements. In order to maximise your chance of success, you need to make sure you apply to courses that are likely to make you an offer corresponding roughly with the grades you expect to achieve. This issue is examined in greater detail in the next chapter.

Resources

Publications

- *Choosing Your Degree Course & University*, Trotman, www. trotman.co.uk.
- *Getting into the UK's Best Universities and Courses*, Trotman, www.trotman.co.uk.
- *Heap 2014: University Degree Course Offers*, Trotman, www. trotman.co.uk.
- *Insider's Guide to Applying to University*, Trotman, www.trotman. co.uk.
- *The Times Good University Guide*, HarperCollins, www.thetimes. co.uk/tto/public/gug
- *The UCAS Guide to Getting into University and College*, UCAS, www.ucasbooks.com.
- *The Virgin Guide to British Universities*, Virgin Books, www. eburypublishing.co.uk.

Websites

General

- www.ucas.com.
- www.push.co.uk.
- www.guardian.co.uk/education/universityguide.
- www.thetimes.co.uk/tto/public/gug.

For students with disabilities

- www.rnib.org.uk: Royal National Institute of Blind People.
- www.actiononhearingloss.org.uk: Action on Hearing Loss (formerly the Royal National Institute for Deaf People).
- www.disabilityrightsuk.org: Disability Rights UK (information for students with disabilities).

6 | Academic requirements

You may have been thinking since Year 10 or 11 about whether you will be able to fulfil higher education entry requirements, carefully planning how your AS and A levels, Scottish Highers, IB, ILC or BTEC National modules will build a sound educational foundation on which you will be able to progress into higher education. On the other hand, you may not have given the matter any serious thought yet.

It is important to make sure you are realistic about the grades you hope to achieve and that you target your applications accordingly.

This chapter will help you understand how universities and colleges express their entry requirements and offers some basic dos and don'ts relating to the final five courses you select.

What might the entry requirements be?

Would-be higher education entrants normally need to achieve minimum qualifications equivalent to one of the following:

- two A levels
- one Double Award A level
- an Advanced Diploma
- the Cambridge Pre-U
- one BTEC National Award
- two Advanced Highers
- an ILC
- an IB.

See page 50 for a full list.

You will also need supporting GCSEs/S grades at grades A*–C/1–3 (note that requirements vary for mature students and other groups – see page 59).

In reality, however, most universities and colleges require more than the basic minimum and many demand particular subjects for entry.

There are two main reasons for admission to some courses requiring higher than minimum grades.

1. **Coping with the course:** for the study of some subjects, a higher education department or faculty can decide that all its students need to achieve a particular qualification (say, B or C in A level Maths) in order to get through the course.
2. **Rationing places:** where there is high demand for a course the entry requirements will rise, because if a department asks for three Bs, fewer applicants will qualify for entry than if three Cs were requested (even though the three-C candidates might cope perfectly well with the course); grade requirements help to ration places.

The second of these two reasons is the more common – and it's therefore worth being aware that high grades are often an indication of popularity, and not always of quality. Some universities, colleges and courses are more popular than others and can therefore set high grades if they feel that the 'market' in a particular subject will bear them. For example, the universities of Oxford and Cambridge can ask for particularly high levels of performance.

Particularly popular courses for 2012 entry were biological sciences, business and management studies, creative art and design, education, engineering, law, medicine and dentistry, and subjects allied to medicine and physical sciences. According to UCAS, in January 2013 the top five subjects for 2013 entry were, in descending order: nursing, psychology, law, pre-clinical medicine and design studies. In addition, any course with a special feature (such as sponsorship or an exchange with an institution overseas) can attract large numbers of applications and may therefore also require high grades.

Whatever course you apply for, your qualifications are bound to be examined carefully by admissions tutors. They will be looking at your advanced-level study and checking that you are:

- offering the right subjects to satisfy entry requirements
- offering subjects they are prepared to include in an offer
- offering the types of qualification they want (e.g. AS and A level, BTEC National)
- offering the right number of qualifications
- making an effort to fill any gaps in your record (e.g. by retaking GCSE Maths alongside your A levels).

Admissions tutors will be on the lookout for students who are repeating A levels; your UCAS application must give full details of your results at the first attempt and include details of what you are repeating and when (see Chapter 15). Further explanations should be given in your personal statement.

Many admissions tutors will also attach a lot of importance to your results at GCSE or Scottish Standard Grade level and to your AS results. After all, these will usually be the only evidence of your academic achievement to date. Tutors will be looking for:

- a reasonable spread of academic qualifications
- key subjects (e.g. English language and maths – and even if the university or college does not require them, most employers do)
- a sound basis for sixth-form (or equivalent advanced-level) study
- signs of academic capacity or potential.

Additional and alternative entry requirements

Applicants to music, art and design and other creative or performing arts courses often have to compile a portfolio of work, and may also have to attend an audition. (See Chapter 9 for more information.)

Should you wish to train for work with young children or vulnerable adults (for example in teaching, social work or the healthcare professions), the university or college will ask that you agree to have a criminal record check from the Disclosure and Barring Service (created in 2012 from a merger of the Criminal Records Bureau and the Independent Safeguarding Authority), known as a DBS check (see Chapter 12 or www.gov.uk/disclosure-barring-service-check for further details).

Applicants for healthcare courses such as medicine, dentistry, nursing or midwifery are advised to be immunised against hepatitis B and may be asked to supply certificates to show that they are not infected with it. You should check the immunisation requirements with the universities and colleges you have chosen.

If you intend to apply for vocational courses, such as law or veterinary science, work experience may be an essential prerequisite for entry. You should check this well before applying to give you time to acquire it if necessary.

Students with certain disabilities may also be offered different entry requirements – it is worth checking with admissions tutors for individual courses as the criteria for admission may be relaxed.

How are entry requirements expressed?

Entry requirements may be expressed as specific grades (e.g. BBC at A level or ABBB at Scottish Higher), as a target number of UCAS Tariff points (e.g. 280 points) or as a mixture of the two (e.g. 280 points, including at least grade B in A level Chemistry).

TIP!

Entry requirements are listed in each course's entry profile in the UCAS course search. Check these before you apply!

The UCAS Tariff

Admission to higher education courses generally depends on an individual's achievement in level 3 qualifications, such as GCE A levels. Fifty-two of these qualifications are included in the UCAS Tariff (see page 50).

As if the number of qualifications available is not confusing enough, different qualifications can have different grading structures (alphabetical, numerical or a mixture of both). Finding out what qualifications are needed for different higher education courses can be very confusing.

The UCAS Tariff is the system for allocating points to qualifications used for entry to higher education. It allows students to use a range of different qualifications to help secure a place on an undergraduate course.

Some universities and colleges use the UCAS Tariff to make comparisons between applicants with different qualifications. Tariff points are often used in entry requirements, although other factors are often taken into account as well. Entry details (available from UCAS and on the university's own website) provide a fuller picture of what admissions tutors are seeking.

The tables on pages 51–57 show the qualifications covered by the UCAS Tariff. There may have been changes to these tables since this book was printed, so you should visit www.ucas.ac.uk/students/ucas_tariff to view the most up-to-date tables.

TIP!

If you have (or are likely to achieve) less than the minimum qualifications for entry to an honours degree course, your qualification level may be suitable for entry to an HND course or foundation degree, which you can convert into a full degree with an additional year of study (see Chapter 4 for further information).

Further information

Although Tariff points can be accumulated in a variety of ways, not all of these will necessarily be acceptable for entry to a particular higher education course. The achievement of a points score does not, therefore, give an automatic entitlement to entry, and many other factors are taken into account in the admissions process. The UCAS course search tool at www.ucas.com is the best source of reference for which qualifications are acceptable for entry to specific courses.

How does the Tariff work?

- Students can collect Tariff points from a range of different qualifications, e.g. GCE A level with BTEC Nationals.
- There is no ceiling to the number of points that can be accumulated.

- There is no double counting. Certain qualifications in the Tariff build on qualifications in the same subject that also attract Tariff points. In these cases, only the qualification with the higher Tariff score will be counted. This principle applies to:
  - BTEC National Award, Certificate and Diploma (NQF)
  - BTEC National Certificate, Subsidiary Diploma, Diploma and Extended Diploma (QCF)
  - CACHE Award, Certificate and Diploma in Child Care and Education
  - Essential Skills Wales at levels 2 and 3
  - GCE Advanced Subsidiary level and GCE Advanced level
  - OCR iMedia level 3 Certificate and Diploma
  - Irish Leaving Certificate at Ordinary and Higher levels
  - OCR iPRO Certificate and Diploma
  - Key Skills at levels 2, 3 and 4
  - OCR National Certificate, Diploma and Advanced Diploma
  - Scottish Highers and Advanced Highers
  - speech, drama and music awards at grades 6, 7 and 8.
- UCAS Tariff points are allocated to level 2 qualifications only if both the following criteria are met:
  - they are broad skills qualifications: Core Skills, Essential Skills, Functional Skills or Key Skills
  - they are being studied as part of a wider composite qualification, such as 14–19 Diplomas or Welsh Baccalaureate.
- Tariff points for the Advanced Diploma come from the Progression Diploma score plus the relevant Additional and Specialist Learning (ASL) Tariff points. Please see the appropriate qualification in the Tariff tables to calculate the ASL score.
- The Extended Project Tariff points are included in the Tariff points for Progression and Advanced Diplomas. Extended Project points represented in the Tariff count only when the qualification is taken outside these Diplomas.
- Where the Tariff tables refer to specific awarding organisations, only qualifications from these awarding bodies attract Tariff points.
- Qualifications with a similar title but from a different qualification-awarding body do not attract Tariff points.

How does higher education use the Tariff?

The Tariff provides a facility to assist higher education institutions when expressing entrance requirements and when making conditional offers. Entry requirements and conditional offers expressed as Tariff points will often require a minimum level of achievement in a specified subject (for example '300 points to include grade A at A level Chemistry', or '260 points including SQA Higher grade B in Mathematics'). Use of the Tariff may also vary from department to department at any one institution, and may in some cases depend on the programme being offered.

WHAT QUALIFICATIONS ARE INCLUDED IN THE TARIFF?

The following qualifications are included in the UCAS Tariff. See the number on the qualification title to find the relevant section of the Tariff table.

1 AAT NVQ Level 3 in Accounting
2 AAT Level 3 Diploma in Accounting (QCF)
3 Advanced Diploma
4 Advanced Extension Awards
5 Advanced Placement Programme (US and Canada)
6 Arts Award (Gold)
7 ASDAN Community Volunteering qualification
8 Asset Languages Advanced Stage
9 British Horse Society (Stage 3 Horse Knowledge & Care, Stage 3 Riding and Preliminary Teacher's Certificate)
10 BTEC Awards (NQF)
11 BTEC Certificates and Extended Certificates (NQF)
12 BTEC Diplomas (NQF)
13 BTEC National in Early Years (NQF)
14 BTEC Nationals (NQF)
15 BTEC QCF Qualifications (Suite known as Nationals)
16 BTEC Specialist Qualifications (QCF)
17 CACHE Award, Certificate and Diploma in Child Care and Education
18 CACHE Level 3 Extended Diploma for the Children and Young People's Workforce (QCF)
19 Cambridge ESOL Examinations
20 Cambridge Pre-U
21 Certificate of Personal Effectiveness (COPE)
22 CISI Introduction to Securities and Investment
23 City & Guilds Land Based Services Level 3 Qualifications
24 Graded Dance and Vocational Graded Dance
25 Diploma in Fashion Retail
26 Diploma in Foundation Studies (Art & Design; Art, Design & Media)
27 EDI Level 3 Certificate in Accounting, Certificate in Accounting (IAS)
28 Essential Skills (Northern Ireland)
29 Essential Skills Wales
30 Extended Project (stand alone)
31 Free-standing Mathematics
32 Functional skills
33 GCE (AS, AS Double Award, A level, A level Double Award and A level (with additional AS))
34 Hong Kong Diploma of Secondary Education (from 2012 entry onwards)
35 ifs School of Finance (Certificate and Diploma in Financial Studies)
36 iMedia (OCR level Certificate/Diploma for iMedia Professionals)
37 International Baccalaureate (IB) Diploma
38 International Baccalaureate (IB) Certificate
39 Irish Leaving Certificate (Higher and Ordinary levels)
40 IT Professionals (iPRO) (Certificate and Diploma)
41 Key Skills (Levels 2, 3 and 4)
42 Music examinations (grades 6, 7 and 8)
43 OCR Level 3 Certificate in Mathematics for Engineering
44 OCR Level 3 Certificate for Young Enterprise
45 OCR Nationals (National Certificate, National Diploma and National Extended Diploma)
46 Principal Learning Wales
47 Progression Diploma
48 Rockschool Music Practitioners Qualifications
49 Scottish Qualifications
50 Speech and Drama examinations (grades 6, 7 and 8 and Performance Studies)
51 Sports Leaders UK
52 Welsh Baccalaureate Advanced Diploma (Core)

Updates on the Tariff, including details on the incorporation of any new qualifications, are posted on **www.ucas.com**.

UCAS TARIFF TABLES

1

AAT NVQ LEVEL 3 IN ACCOUNTING	
GRADE	TARIFF POINTS
PASS	160

2

AAT LEVEL 3 DIPLOMA IN ACCOUNTING	
GRADE	TARIFF POINTS
PASS	160

3

ADVANCED DIPLOMA

Advanced Diploma = Progression Diploma plus Additional & Specialist Learning (ASL). Please see the appropriate qualification to calculate the ASL score. Please see the Progression Diploma (Table 47) for Tariff scores

4

ADVANCED EXTENSION AWARDS	
GRADE	TARIFF POINTS
DISTINCTION	40
MERIT	20

Points for Advanced Extension Awards are over and above those gained from the A level grade

5

ADVANCED PLACEMENT PROGRAMME (US & CANADA)	
GRADE	TARIFF POINTS
Group A	
5	120
4	90
3	60
Group B	
5	50
4	35
3	20

Details of the subjects covered by each group can be found at www.ucas.com/students/ucas_tariff/tarifftables

6

ARTS AWARD (GOLD)	
GRADE	TARIFF POINTS
PASS	35

7

ASDAN COMMUNITY VOLUNTEERING QUALIFICATION	
GRADE	TARIFF POINTS
CERTIFICATE	50
AWARD	30

8

ASSET LANGUAGES ADVANCED STAGE			
GRADE	TARIFF POINTS	GRADE	TARIFF POINTS
Speaking		Listening	
GRADE 12	28	GRADE 12	25
GRADE 11	20	GRADE 11	18
GRADE 10	12	GRADE 10	11
Reading		Writing	
GRADE 12	25	GRADE 12	25
GRADE 11	18	GRADE 11	18
GRADE 10	11	GRADE 10	11

9

BRITISH HORSE SOCIETY	
GRADE	TARIFF POINTS
Stage 3 Horse Knowledge & Care	
PASS	35
Stage 3 Riding	
PASS	35
Preliminary Teacher's Certificate	
PASS	35

Awarded by Equestrian Qualifications (GB) Ltd (EQL)

10

BTEC AWARDS (NQF) (EXCLUDING BTEC NATIONAL QUALIFICATIONS)			
GRADE	TARIFF POINTS		
	Group A	Group B	Group C
DISTINCTION	20	30	40
MERIT	13	20	26
PASS	7	10	13

Details of the subjects covered by each group can be found at www.ucas.com/students/ucas_tariff/tarifftables

11

BTEC CERTIFICATES AND EXTENDED CERTIFICATES (NQF) (EXCLUDING BTEC NATIONAL QUALIFICATIONS)					
GRADE	TARIFF POINTS				
	Group A	Group B	Group C	Group D	Extended Certificates
DISTINCTION	40	60	80	100	60
MERIT	26	40	52	65	40
PASS	13	20	26	35	20

Details of the subjects covered by each group can be found at www.ucas.com/students/ucas_tariff/tarifftables

12

BTEC DIPLOMAS (NQF) (EXCLUDING BTEC NATIONAL QUALIFICATIONS)			
GRADE	TARIFF POINTS		
	Group A	Group B	Group C
DISTINCTION	80	100	120
MERIT	52	65	80
PASS	26	35	40

Details of the subjects covered by each group can be found at www.ucas.com/students/ucas_tariff/tarifftables

UCAS TARIFF TABLES

13

BTEC NATIONAL IN EARLY YEARS (NQF)

GRADE	TARIFF POINTS	GRADE	TARIFF POINTS	GRADE	TARIFF POINTS
Theory		Certificate		Practical	
Diploma				D	120
DDD	320	DD	200	M	80
DDM	280	DM	160	P	40
DMM	240	MM	120		
MMM	220	MP	80		
MMP	160	PP	40		
MPP	120				
PPP	80				

Points apply to the following qualifications only: BTEC National Diploma in Early Years (100/1279/5); BTEC National Certificate in Early Years (100/1280/1)

14

BTEC NATIONALS (NQF)

GRADE	TARIFF POINTS	GRADE	TARIFF POINTS	GRADE	TARIFF POINTS
Diploma		Certificate		Award	
DDD	360	DD	240	D	120
DDM	320	DM	200	M	80
DMM	280	MM	160	P	40
MMM	240	MP	120		
MMP	200	PP	80		
MPP	160				
PPP	120				

15

BTEC QUALIFICATIONS (QCF) (SUITE OF QUALIFICATIONS KNOWN AS NATIONALS)

EXTENDED DIPLOMA	DIPLOMA	90 CREDIT DIPLOMA	SUBSIDIARY DIPLOMA	CERTIFICATE	TARIFF POINTS
D*D*D*					420
D*D*D					400
D*DD					380
DDD					360
DDM					320
DMM	D*D*				280
	D*D				260
MMM	DD				240
		D*D*			210
MMP	DM	D*D			200
		DD			180
MPP	MM	DM			160
			D*		140
PPP	MP	MM	D		120
		MP			100
	PP		M		80
			D*		70
		PP		D	60
			P	M	40
				P	20

16

BTEC SPECIALIST (QCF)

GRADE	TARIFF POINTS		
	Diploma	Certificate	Award
DISTINCTION	120	60	20
MERIT	80	40	13
PASS	40	20	7

17

CACHE LEVEL 3 AWARD, CERTIFICATE AND DIPLOMA IN CHILD CARE & EDUCATION					
AWARD		CERTIFICATE		DIPLOMA	
GRADE	TARIFF POINTS	GRADE	TARIFF POINTS	GRADE	TARIFF POINTS
A	30	A	110	A	360
B	25	B	90	B	300
C	20	C	70	C	240
D	15	D	55	D	180
E	10	E	35	E	120

18

CACHE LEVEL 3 EXTENDED DIPLOMA FOR THE CHILDREN AND YOUNG PEOPLE'S WORKFORCE (QCF)	
GRADE	TARIFF POINTS
A*	420
A	340
B	290
C	240
D	140
E	80

19

CAMBRIDGE ESOL EXAMINATIONS	
GRADE	TARIFF POINTS
Certificate of Proficiency in English	
A	140
B	110
C	70
Certificate in Advanced English	
A	70

20

CAMBRIDGE PRE-U							
GRADE	TARIFF POINTS	GRADE	TARIFF POINTS	GRADE	TARIFF POINTS	GRADE	TARIFF POINTS
Principal Subject		Global Perspectives and Research		Short Course			
D1	TBC	D1	TBC	D1	TBC		
D2	145	D2	140	D2	TBC		
D3	130	D3	126	D3	60		
M1	115	M1	112	M1	53		
M2	101	M2	98	M2	46		
M3	87	M3	84	M3	39		
P1	73	P1	70	P1	32		
P2	59	P2	56	P2	26		
P3	46	P3	42	P3	20		

21

CERTIFICATE OF PERSONAL EFFECTIVENESS (COPE)	
GRADE	TARIFF POINTS
PASS	70

Points are awarded for the Certificate of Personal Effectiveness (CoPE) awarded by ASDAN and CCEA

22

CISI INTRODUCTION TO SECURITIES AND INVESTMENT	
GRADE	TARIFF POINTS
PASS WITH DISTINCTION	60
PASS WITH MERIT	40
PASS	20

23

CITY AND GUILDS LAND BASED SERVICES LEVEL 3 QUALIFICATIONS				
GRADE	TARIFF POINTS			
	EXTENDED DIPLOMA	DIPLOMA	SUBSIDIARY DIPLOMA	CERTIFICATE
DISTINCTION*	420	280	140	70
DISTINCTION	360	240	120	60
MERIT	240	160	80	40
PASS	120	80	40	20

24

GRADED DANCE AND VOCATIONAL GRADED DANCE					
GRADE	TARIFF POINTS	GRADE	TARIFF POINTS	GRADE	TARIFF POINTS
Graded Dance					
Grade 8		Grade 7		Grade 6	
DISTINCTION	65	DISTINCTION	55	DISTINCTION	40
MERIT	55	MERIT	45	MERIT	35
PASS	45	PASS	35	PASS	30
Vocational Graded Dance					
Advanced Foundation		Intermediate			
DISTINCTION	70	DISTINCTION	65		
MERIT	55	MERIT	50		
PASS	45	PASS	40		

25

DIPLOMA IN FASHION RETAIL	
GRADE	TARIFF POINTS
DISTINCTION	160
MERIT	120
PASS	80

Applies to the NQF and QCF versions of the qualifications awarded by ABC Awards

How to Complete Your UCAS Application

26

DIPLOMA IN FOUNDATION STUDIES (ART & DESIGN AND ART, DESIGN & MEDIA)

GRADE	TARIFF POINTS
DISTINCTION	285
MERIT	225
PASS	165

Awarded by ABC, Edexcel, UAL and WJEC

27

EDI LEVEL 3 CERTIFICATE IN ACCOUNTING, CERTIFICATE IN ACCOUNTING (IAS)

GRADE	TARIFF POINTS
DISTINCTION	120
MERIT	90
PASS	70

28

ESSENTIAL SKILLS (NORTHERN IRELAND)

GRADE	TARIFF POINTS
LEVEL 2	10

Only allocated at level 2 if studied as part of a wider composite qualification such as 14-19 Diploma or Welsh Baccalaureate

29

ESSENTIAL SKILLS WALES

GRADE	TARIFF POINTS
LEVEL 4	30
LEVEL 3	20
LEVEL 2	10

Only allocated at level 2 if studied as part of a wider composite qualification such as 14-19 Diploma or Welsh Baccalaureate

30

EXTENDED PROJECT (STAND ALONE)

GRADE	TARIFF POINTS
A*	70
A	60
B	50
C	40
D	30
E	20

Points for the Extended Project cannot be counted if taken as part of Progression/Advanced Diploma

31

FREE-STANDING MATHEMATICS

GRADE	TARIFF POINTS
A	20
B	17
C	13
D	10
E	7

Covers free-standing Mathematics - Additional Maths, Using and Applying Statistics, Working with Algebraic and Graphical Techniques, Modelling with Calculus

32

FUNCTIONAL SKILLS

GRADE	TARIFF POINTS
LEVEL 2	10

Only allocated if studied as part of a wider composite qualification such as 14-19 Diploma or Welsh Baccalaureate

33

GCE AND VCE

GRADE	TARIFF POINTS	GRADE	TARIFF POINTS	GRADE	TARIFF POINTS	GRADE	TARIFF POINTS	GRADE	TARIFF POINTS
GCE & AVCE Double Award		GCE A level with additional AS (9 units)		GCE A level & AVCE		GCE AS Double Award		GCE AS & AS VCE	
A*A*	280	A*A	200	A*	140	AA	120	A	60
A*A	260	AA	180	A	120	AB	110	B	50
AA	240	AB	170	B	100	BB	100	C	40
AB	220	BB	150	C	80	BC	90	D	30
BB	200	BC	140	D	60	CC	80	E	20
BC	180	CC	120	E	40	CD	70		
CC	160	CD	110			DD	60		
CD	140	DD	90			DE	50		
DD	120	DE	80			EE	40		
DE	100	EE	60						
EE	80								

34

HONG KONG DIPLOMA OF SECONDARY EDUCATION

GRADE	TARIFF POINTS	GRADE	TARIFF POINTS	GRADE	TARIFF POINTS
All subjects except mathematics		Mathematics compulsory component		Mathematics optional components	
5**	No value	5**	No value	5**	No value
5*	130	5*	60	5*	70
5	120	5	45	5	60
4	80	4	35	4	50
3	40	3	25	3	40

No value for 5** pending receipt of candidate evidence (post 2012)

35

IFS SCHOOL OF FINANCE (NQF & QCF)			
GRADE	TARIFF POINTS	GRADE	TARIFF POINTS
Certificate in Financial Studies (CeFS)		Diploma in Financial Studies (DipFS)	
A	60	A	120
B	50	B	100
C	40	C	80
D	30	D	60
E	20	E	40

Applicants with the ifs Diploma cannot also count points allocated to the ifs Certificate. Completion of both qualifications will result in a maximum of 120 UCAS Tariff points

36

LEVEL 3 CERTIFICATE / DIPLOMA FOR iMEDIA USERS (iMEDIA)	
GRADE	TARIFF POINTS
DIPLOMA	66
CERTIFICATE	40

Awarded by OCR

37

INTERNATIONAL BACCALAUREATE (IB) DIPLOMA			
GRADE	TARIFF POINTS	GRADE	TARIFF POINTS
45	720	34	479
44	698	33	457
43	676	32	435
42	654	31	413
41	632	30	392
40	611	29	370
39	589	28	348
38	567	27	326
37	545	26	304
36	523	25	282
35	501	24	260

38

INTERNATIONAL BACCALAUREATE (IB) CERTIFICATE					
GRADE	TARIFF POINTS	GRADE	TARIFF POINTS	GRADE	TARIFF POINTS
Higher Level		Standard Level		Core	
7	130	7	70	3	120
6	110	6	59	2	80
5	80	5	43	1	40
4	50	4	27	0	10
3	20	3	11		

39

IRISH LEAVING CERTIFICATE			
GRADE	TARIFF POINTS	GRADE	TARIFF POINTS
Higher		Ordinary	
A1	90	A1	39
A2	77	A2	26
B1	71	B1	20
B2	64	B2	14
B3	58	B3	7
C1	52		
C2	45		
C3	39		
D1	33		
D2	26		
D3	20		

40

IT PROFESSIONALS (iPRO)	
GRADE	TARIFF POINTS
DIPLOMA	100
CERTIFICATE	80

Awarded by OCR

41

KEY SKILLS	
GRADE	TARIFF POINTS
LEVEL 4	30
LEVEL 3	20
LEVEL 2	10

Only allocated at level 2 if studied as part of a wider composite qualification such as 14-19 Diploma or Welsh Baccalaureate

How to Complete Your UCAS Application

42

MUSIC EXAMINATIONS					
GRADE	TARIFF POINTS	GRADE	TARIFF POINTS	GRADE	TARIFF POINTS
Practical					
Grade 8		Grade 7		Grade 6	
DISTINCTION	75	DISTINCTION	60	DISTINCTION	45
MERIT	70	MERIT	55	MERIT	40
PASS	55	PASS	40	PASS	25
Theory					
Grade 8		Grade 7		Grade 6	
DISTINCTION	30	DISTINCTION	20	DISTINCTION	15
MERIT	25	MERIT	15	MERIT	10
PASS	20	PASS	10	PASS	5

Points shown are for the ABRSM, LCMM/University of West London, Rockschool and Trinity Guildhall/Trinity College London Advanced Level music examinations

43

OCR LEVEL 3 CERTIFICATE IN MATHEMATICS FOR ENGINEERING	
GRADE	TARIFF POINTS
A*	TBC
A	90
B	75
C	60
D	45
E	30

44

OCR LEVEL 3 CERTIFICATE FOR YOUNG ENTERPRISE	
GRADE	TARIFF POINTS
DISTINCTION	40
MERIT	30
PASS	20

45

OCR NATIONALS							
GRADE	TARIFF POINTS	GRADE	TARIFF POINTS	GRADE	TARIFF POINTS	GRADE	TARIFF POINTS
National Extended Diploma		National Diploma		National Certificate			
D1	360	D	240	D	120		
D2/M1	320	M1	200	M	80		
M2	280	M2/P1	160	P	40		
M3	240	P2	120				
P1	200	P3	80				
P2	160						
P3	120						

46

PRINCIPAL LEARNING WALES	
GRADE	TARIFF POINTS
A*	210
A	180
B	150
C	120
D	90
E	60

47

PROGRESSION DIPLOMA	
GRADE	TARIFF POINTS
A*	350
A	300
B	250
C	200
D	150
E	100

Advanced Diploma = Progression Diploma plus Additional & Specialist Learning (ASL). Please see the appropriate qualification to calculate the ASL score

48

GRADE	ROCKSCHOOL MUSIC PRACTITIONERS QUALIFICATIONS				
	TARIFF POINTS				
	Extended Diploma	Diploma	Subsidiary Diploma	Extended Certificate	Certificate
DISTINCTION	240	180	120	60	30
MERIT	160	120	80	40	20
PASS	80	60	40	20	10

49

SCOTTISH QUALIFICATIONS							
GRADE	TARIFF POINTS	GRADE	TARIFF POINTS	GRADE	TARIFF POINTS	GROUP	TARIFF POINTS
Advanced Higher		Higher		Scottish Interdisciplinary Project		Scottish National Certificates	
A	130	A	80	A	65	C	125
B	110	B	65	B	55	B	100
C	90	C	50	C	45	A	75
D	72	D	36				
Ungraded Higher		NPA PC Passport					
PASS	45	PASS	45				
		Core Skills					
		HIGHER	20				

Details of the subjects covered by each Scottish National Certificate can be found at www.ucas.com/students/ucas_tariff/tarifftables

50

SPEECH AND DRAMA EXAMINATIONS							
GRADE	TARIFF POINTS	GRADE	TARIFF POINTS	GRADE	TARIFF POINTS	GRADE	TARIFF POINTS
PCertLAM		Grade 8		Grade 7		Grade 6	
DISTINCTION	90	DISTINCTION	65	DISTINCTION	55	DISTINCTION	40
MERIT	80	MERIT	60	MERIT	50	MERIT	35
PASS	60	PASS	45	PASS	35	PASS	20

Details of the Speech and Drama Qualifications covered by the Tariff can be found at www.ucas.com/students/ucas_tariff/tarifftables

51

SPORTS LEADERS UK	
GRADE	TARIFF POINTS
PASS	30

These points are awarded to Higher Sports Leader Award and Level 3 Certificate in Higher Sports Leadership (QCF)

52

WELSH BACCALAUREATE ADVANCED DIPLOMA (CORE)	
GRADE	TARIFF POINTS
PASS	120

These points are awarded only when a candidate achieves the Welsh Baccalaureate Advanced Diploma

Unit grade information

As a result of the increasing need to differentiate between the many well-qualified applicants for higher education, unit grade information for certificated qualifications (such as GCE AS and A level) will be supplied to universities and colleges. This is intended to give them greater depth of information about applicants, in order to help them decide whether to make an offer and to assess applicants' strengths and weaknesses. This means that the grades you achieve in each unit of your qualification, as well as your final overall grade, may start to matter. There is space for you to fill in your unit grade scores on your UCAS application, and the information will also be made available by UCAS direct to institutions. Unit grades may be specified as part of conditional offers, but it is not expected that this practice will be widespread.

You should look at individual university and college prospectuses and websites and check entry requirements and profiles to find out their individual policies relating to unit grade information.

Subjects

It is very important to check the combination of advanced-level subjects that is acceptable for admission to particular courses. Some departments prefer the more traditional A level, Scottish Higher and IB subjects for the minimum entry requirement to some courses. There are no standard university-wide lists available, so the only way to clarify this is by consulting the admissions requirements for the course you would like to do.

Generally speaking, if you are taking two or more of the following subjects at advanced level, you should check that the combination will be acceptable:

- accounting
- art and design
- business studies
- communication studies
- dance
- design and technology
- drama and theatre studies
- film studies
- general studies
- health and social care
- home economics
- information and communication technology
- information technology in a global society
- leisure studies
- media studies
- music technology
- performance studies

- performing arts
- photography
- physical education
- sports studies
- theatre arts
- travel and tourism
- visual arts
- world development.

Mature students

There is no single definition of a 'mature' applicant, but most universities and colleges now classify students as mature if they are over 21 years of age (or 20 in Scotland) at the date of entry to a course. The vast majority of departments welcome applications from mature students, and many, especially science departments, would like more.

As a mature student, you are more likely to be accepted with qualifications that would not be enough if they were presented by a student aged 18 who is in full-time education. That said, there is still fierce competition for places, and in most subjects places are not set aside for mature students. If you are considered favourably, you are likely to be called for interview. It is not usually advisable to rely only on qualifications gained several years ago at school; university and college departments will want to see recent evidence of your academic ability so that they can evaluate your application fairly. In addition, taking a course of study at the right level helps prepare you for full-time student life.

For these reasons, entry requirements for mature students are difficult to quantify, but a good approach might be to go to a further education college and study for one of the usual post-16 qualifications (e.g. an A level or BTEC National Award) or to take one of the Access to Higher Education or foundation courses specially designed for mature students. You may also find that you can get Accreditation of Prior Learning (APL) to recognise the skills you have developed in the workplace – see the UCAS website listed in the 'Resources' section at the end of this chapter for more information.

TIP!

It is advisable for mature students to contact departments directly to ask about their admissions policies before applying to UCAS and to tailor their applications accordingly.

Targeting the right courses

Here are a few dos and don'ts to make sure that the final five courses you select are targeted to give you the best chance of success.

Do . . .

- Carefully check the required entry grades and qualifications on the UCAS website, then confirm them by checking the universities' or colleges' prospectuses or websites or, preferably, by contacting them directly to ensure that there is no chance you have misunderstood or that any changes have been made since the prospectuses were printed.
- Check that the post-16 qualifications you have opted to take will give you the entry qualifications you need and that you are on track to achieve the right grades.
- Be realistic about the grades you are likely to achieve.
- As a safety net, make sure you apply to at least one institution that is likely to give you a slightly lower offer.

Don't . . .

- Apply for lots of different or unrelated subjects: you will have a difficult job justifying this in your personal statement, and admissions tutors will question how genuine your interest is in each subject.
- Even if you expect high grades, think very carefully before applying to five very popular universities for a very popular subject. Entry will be extremely competitive and, even with high predicted grades, you cannot be sure of being accepted. Better to include at least one university or college that is not so oversubscribed, and therefore makes offers at a slightly lower level.

Resources

Publications

- *Choosing Your Degree Course & University*, Trotman, www. trotman.co.uk.
- *Heap 2014: University Degree Course Offers*, Trotman, www. trotman.co.uk.

Websites

- www.ucas.com/students/choosingcourses.

- www.gov.uk/disclosure-barring-service-check: DBS checks in England and Wales.
- www.disclosurescotland.co.uk: criminal record checks in Scotland.
- www.dojni.gov.uk/accessni: criminal record checks in Northern Ireland.
- www.materials.ac.uk/resources/library/apelintro.asp: information about Accreditation of Prior and Experiential Learning (APEL), including a downloadable document.

Part II

The admissions procedure: applications, interviews, offers and beyond

7 | Applications and offers

Making your application

As the timetable on pages 3–6 shows, if you are on a two-year advanced course, all your higher education research work should ideally be done by September or October of the second year – more than a year before you start in higher education.

If you are on a one-year course, you won't have time to do all the activities suggested for the first year, but you are working to the same application deadlines and you still need to research all your options.

UCAS applicant journey

The UCAS applicant journey (see Figure 1, page 66) has been designed to guide you through the different steps you will take when making your application for higher education.

Deadlines

There are three deadlines for applications to courses through UCAS: 15 October, 15 January and 24 March.

The deadline for application to most courses is 15 January. (Remember, however, that you will have to submit your application to your referee well before this.) All applications submitted by 15 January are considered – however, it is advisable to apply as early as you can. This is because too many people apply after Christmas, during the two weeks leading up to the 15 January deadline; those who apply earlier may therefore receive a quicker decision simply because smaller numbers are being handled. Aim to submit your UCAS application to your referee by late November or by any internal deadline given by your school or college.

Some courses have an earlier application deadline:

- applications for courses leading to professional qualifications in medicine, dentistry or veterinary science/medicine must be submitted by 15 October
- applications for all courses at the universities of Oxford or Cambridge must be submitted by 15 October.

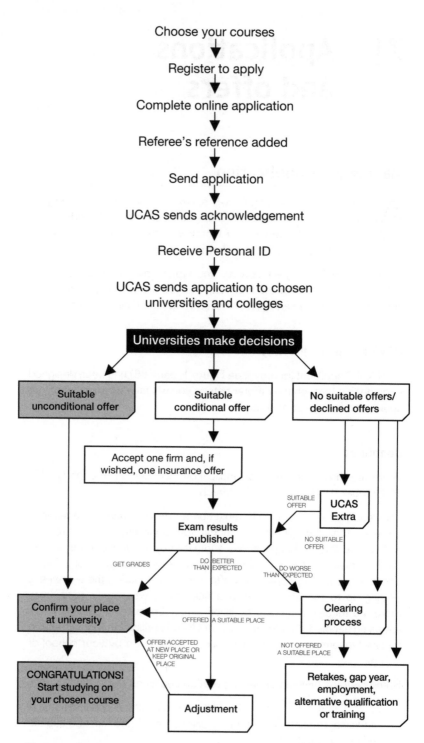

Figure 1 Applicant journey

Some subjects have a later deadline:

- the deadline for the receipt at UCAS of applications for art and design courses, except those listed with a 15 January deadline, is 24 March. (If you apply for art and design courses with different deadlines, you can submit your application before 15 January for courses with that deadline, then add further choices before the 24 March deadline, unless you have already used all five choices.)

What happens once you submit your application?

UCAS will send you a welcome letter acknowledging receipt of your application and confirming your personal details and the courses you have applied for. You must check that this information is correct, and contact the UCAS Customer Contact Centre immediately if it is not (0871 486 0468, between 8.30a.m. and 6p.m., Monday to Friday).

UCAS will also provide you with your Track Personal ID. Along with the password and username you used for Apply (see Chapter 11), this will enable you to log in to the UCAS database and use Track (the online tracking system) to follow the progress of your application. Keep a careful note of your Personal ID and, if you contact UCAS, universities or colleges, be prepared to quote it – this will save a lot of time and trouble.

Admissions tutors can now look at your application and decide whether or not to make you an offer.

Decisions and offers

Universities and colleges will inform UCAS of their decisions. You should log on to Track periodically to check the status of your application. If you have entered a valid email address, UCAS will email you to tell you that a change has been made to your application status. The message will not specify whether you have received an offer or a rejection, but will ask you to log on to Track to find out.

Decisions will arrive in a random order, possibly beginning a few weeks after you apply. You can also check your offers via Track on the UCAS website. Decisions will be displayed there as soon as UCAS receives them. If you have a long wait, it may mean that you are regarded as a borderline applicant (although this is not always the case).

There are three main categories of decision.

1. **Unconditional offer:** no further qualifications are required. If you accept this offer, you are in!
2. **Conditional offer:** you still have some work to do . . . but if you accept the offer and achieve the conditions in the examinations you are about to take, a place will be guaranteed.

3. **Unsuccessful:** sorry – no place for you.

The following decisions may also appear:

- withdrawn: you have withdrawn this choice
- cancelled: you have asked UCAS to cancel this choice.

Universities and colleges have to decide by 9 May whether or not to offer you a place, provided you applied by the deadline of 15 January. (They are encouraged to make their decision by 31 March.)

Interviews and open days

Before they make a decision, admissions tutors may wish to call you for interview. You should therefore be prepared to travel to universities or colleges during the late autumn and winter; a 16–25 Railcard or a National Express Young Persons Coachcard might be a good investment.

Some universities and colleges will contact you directly to invite you for interview. Others will inform you of interview details through Track on the UCAS website. If you have provided a valid email address on your application and you are invited for interview through Track, UCAS will send you an email asking you to look at the change to your application record in Track. You can accept the interview invitation, decline it or request an alternative date or time in Track.

If you need to change the interview time or date, you should also contact the university or college direct. They can then update the invitation so that the revised details are shown in Track. You should try to attend interviews on the first date given as it may be difficult for universities to offer an alternative date.

Advice on preparing for interviews is given in Chapter 9.

Alternatively, you may be offered a conditional or unconditional place and invited to attend an open day. You might also be asked to submit a portfolio or piece of written work as an alternative.

Replying to offers

You will be asked to reply to any offers you receive – and you must do so – but you do not have to reply until you have received decisions from all of the universities and colleges to which you applied.

You can reply to your offers using Track on the UCAS website. You must reply to each offer with one of three options.

1. **Firm acceptance:** if you firmly accept an offer (either as an unconditional offer or as a conditional offer), this means that you are sure

that this offer is your first preference of all the offers you have received through UCAS. If you get the grades, this will be the higher education course you take. You can make this reply only once; you will not subsequently be able to change or cancel your reply. There is also an equal commitment on the university's or college's part to accept you if you fulfil the conditions.

2. **Insurance acceptance:** if you have firmly accepted a conditional offer, you may also hold one additional offer (either conditional or unconditional) as an insurance acceptance. This is your fall-back, in case your grades are too low for your firm acceptance. It is worth knowing that you are not obliged to make an insurance reply; if you do so and then your firm acceptance offer is not confirmed, you will be expected to attend your insurance choice if that is confirmed. You might feel that you would prefer to wait and see what is available in Extra or Clearing. Please ask for advice before making this decision!

3. **Decline:** if you decline an offer, you are indicating that you definitely do not wish to accept it.

You must either accept or decline your offers. You can accept two offers (your firm and insurance choices) and must decline all your other offers so your combination of replies will be one of the following:

- accept one offer firmly (unconditional firm or conditional firm) and decline any others
- accept one offer firmly (conditional firm) and one as an insurance (unconditional insurance or conditional insurance), and decline any others
- decline all offers.

If you firmly accept an unconditional offer of a place, you are not entitled to choose an insurance offer.

If you firmly accept a conditional offer, you may accept an unconditional offer or another conditional offer as your insurance acceptance.

Tips on making your replies

- Consider your replies very carefully. Ask for advice from your school/college tutor or careers adviser.
- Do not accept an offer (firm or insurance) unless you are sure that you will be happy to enrol on the course. The decisions you make are binding; you are not permitted to alter your choices at a later stage *unless* you find that you have done better than you expected at exam results time and have higher grades than those required by your firm choice. You may choose then to use Adjustment (see Chapter 10).

- It is advisable to choose an unconditional offer as your insurance acceptance or one with conditions that are easier for you to meet than those of your firm acceptance.
- Do not include as an insurance acceptance a course that you would be unwilling to take up. If you are not accepted for your firm choice and the insurance offer is confirmed, you are committed to going there. It would be better not to hold an insurance acceptance than to hold one you would not be willing to take up.
- Bear in mind the precise requirements of the offer. For example, if a BCC offer requires a B in a subject you are not very confident about, whereas an offer requiring higher grades overall does not specify the B in that subject, or perhaps counts general studies, then your firm/insurance decision needs to take these factors into account.

What if you don't get any offers?

If you are in this position, you may be able to make a further application in Extra between the end of February and the end of June. In 2012, 7,859 students were accepted through Extra.

You will be eligible to use Extra if you have used all five choices in your original application and you fulfil any one of the following criteria:

- you have had unsuccessful or withdrawn decisions for all of your choices
- you have cancelled your outstanding choices and hold no offers
- you have received decisions from all five choices and have declined all offers made to you.

If you are eligible, UCAS will notify you of this. When you log on to Track, you will see that a special Extra button becomes available on your screen. Courses that still have vacancies will be searchable in the study options section of the UCAS search tool on the website.

When you enter the Extra course details on your Track screen, your application is automatically sent online to the relevant university or college.

If you are made an offer, you can then choose whether or not to accept it. If you are currently studying for examinations, any offer that you receive is likely to be a conditional one and will contain the required exam grades. If you decide to accept a conditional offer, you will not be able to take any further part in Extra. (There are no insurance options in Extra.) If you already have your exam results, you may receive an unconditional offer. Once you accept an unconditional offer, you have that place.

If you are unsuccessful, decline an offer or do not receive an offer *within 21 days of choosing a course* through Extra, you can (time permitting) make a further application in Extra. The Extra button on your Track screen will be re-activated.

Tips on applying via Extra

- Do some careful research and seek guidance from your school, college or careers adviser and from the universities and colleges themselves.
- Think very carefully before applying again for the types of course for which you have already been unsuccessful – it may simply result in another rejection.
- Be flexible – for example, if you applied to high-demand courses and universities and colleges in your original application and were unsuccessful, you could consider related or alternative subjects.
- If you still do not succeed, you may be able to find a place through Clearing.

8 | Non-standard applications

Applications for the majority of courses follow the pattern outlined in the previous chapters. However, there are some exceptions, specifically for:

- courses at the universities of Oxford and Cambridge
- music conservatoires
- medicine, dentistry and veterinary science or medicine courses
- deferred entry
- late applications.

Oxford and Cambridge

If you intend to apply for any course at either Oxford or Cambridge, the deadline for submitting your application is 15 October 2013. (Earlier dates apply if you wish to be considered for a music or choral scholarship at either university. You can find details on their websites.)

Applicants to Cambridge *from outside the EU only* must submit a Cambridge Online Preliminary Application (COPA) form as well as a UCAS application – and if they wish to be interviewed in certain other countries rather than come to Cambridge they must consult the list of dates on the website. The COPA must also be completed by anyone wishing to be considered for an organ scholarship.

Applicants to the University of Oxford are not required to submit a separate form, but extra information is required for some international interviews.

You can apply to only one course at *either* the University of Oxford or the University of Cambridge. You cannot apply to both universities. There is only one exception to this: if you will be a graduate at the start of the course and are applying for course code A101 (graduate medicine) at the University of Cambridge, you can also apply to medicine (course code A100) at Cambridge, in addition to being able to apply to graduate medicine (course code A101) at the University of Oxford. No other combinations are permitted.

Some applicants will need to complete an additional application form in order to apply. For full information about applying to the

Universities of Oxford or Cambridge, please visit their websites at www.ox.ac.uk/admissions/undergraduate_courses or www.study.cam. ac.uk/undergraduate. In-depth advice on making applications to these universities is also given in *Getting into Oxford & Cambridge* (Trotman Publishing).

Music conservatoires

You can apply for courses at eight UK music conservatoires online using the Conservatoires UK Admissions Service (CUKAS), which is run by UCAS and works in a similar way. However, CUKAS applicants can select six courses rather than the five possible through UCAS.

The eight conservatoires are:

1. Birmingham Conservatoire
2. Leeds College of Music
3. Royal Academy of Music
4. Royal College of Music
5. Royal Northern College of Music
6. Royal Conservatoire of Scotland
7. Royal Welsh College of Music and Drama
8. Trinity Laban Conservatoire of Music and Dance.

You may apply from June 2013 and the application deadline is 1 October 2013, although late entries can be submitted if there are vacancies. Applicants registering on the CUKAS website will be able to access general advice, apply online and track their applications. Further information is available at www.cukas.ac.uk.

Applying to CUKAS does not mean that you are excluded from the UCAS system. The two systems run independently of each other, therefore you may also make up to five UCAS choices.

(Note: the Guildhall School of Music and Drama is a member of Conservatoires UK (the network of British music schools) but is not in the CUKAS system. Applications must be made directly to the school.)

Medicine, dentistry and veterinary science/ veterinary medicine courses

If you intend to apply for a course leading to a professional qualification in medicine, dentistry or veterinary science/medicine, the deadline for submitting your application is 15 October 2013. You are allowed to select a maximum of four courses in any one of these subjects: if you list more than four, Apply (the UCAS application system described fully in Part III) will ask you to reduce your number of choices. The remaining space on your UCAS application can be filled in with a course in another subject, though, should you so wish. There is strong competition for entry to medicine, dentistry and veterinary science/medicine courses and many people are necessarily disappointed in their first choice of study.

In-depth advice on making applications in these subject areas is given in the *Getting into* series (see the 'Resources' section at the end of this chapter).

Deferred entry

Taking a gap year is an increasingly popular option for many students – it offers a unique opportunity to broaden horizons, travel, work as a volunteer and/or (as the cost of higher education continues to rise) save some money while gaining valuable experience in the workplace. If you do plan, for whatever reason, to defer your entry into higher education until 2015, there are three options available to you – each is listed below with a few notes on the pros and cons.

Option 1: apply through UCAS for deferred entry

You can make your application this year (2013/14) and select a start date of 2015 in your UCAS application to indicate that you wish to defer your entry (see Chapter 14). The major advantage of this option is that you get the formalities out of the way while you are still at school or college and available for interview – then you can relax.

Generally speaking, applications for deferred entry are dealt with in the normal way, but do be aware that for some subjects (such as medicine, certain science and maths subjects and professional subjects) admissions tutors may be a little cautious about offering you a place. It is therefore important to be sure you really want to defer before using this option, and to check with the department to which you are thinking of applying whether it would be happy to admit you a year later.

Remember that if you do apply for entry in 2015 but then find that you have no useful way of spending the gap year after all, the institution is not obliged to take you a year earlier (i.e. in 2014). If you choose to defer, remember to mention your reasons and plans for your year out in the personal statement section of Apply (see Chapter 17): this is much more likely to make admissions tutors amenable to giving you a deferred place.

Option 2: apply through UCAS for standard entry

If you are not confident enough of your decision to apply for deferred entry on your UCAS application, you can apply for the normal admission year and, later on, ask the university or college where you are accepted whether you can defer. This means you do not need to say anything on your UCAS application about deferred entry until your plans are really firm – but, on the other hand, the institution is quite entitled to say that the place it has offered you is for 2014 entry only, and you must either take it up or apply all over again for entry in 2015.

Option 3: do not apply through UCAS until the following year

It is possible to delay applying to UCAS until after you have received your results, which means that you make your UCAS application during your gap year. This can be a good option in some instances, especially if your exam results turn out to be significantly different from those that were predicted. Your grades are also guaranteed, and if you accept an offer it will be a firm decision, so universities and colleges may consider you a better bet than a candidate who is only predicted those grades. The disadvantage, though, is that you must find time during your gap year to get your research up to date, fill in your UCAS application and (possibly) attend open days and interviews.

This can limit your gap year options – you will need to be contactable at all times, and flying back from Australia (or wherever else you decide to spend your gap year) to attend an interview could make a serious dent in your finances.

Making a late application

If at all possible, avoid applying late. Many popular courses fill up quickly, and getting a place will be more difficult, if not impossible. However, if you decide you would like to apply to higher education late, you still can. Up to 30 June, UCAS will send your application to your named institutions, but the universities and colleges will consider you only at their discretion. If they do choose to consider you, the same procedures are followed as for a normal application, and you will reply to offers in the usual way. Applications received between 1 July and 20 September will be processed through the Clearing scheme, which operates from mid-July to late September.

Resources

Publications

- *Getting into Art & Design Courses*, Trotman, www.trotman.co.uk.
- *Getting into Dental School*, Trotman, www.trotman.co.uk.
- *Getting into Medical School: 2014 Entry*, Trotman, www.trotman.co.uk.
- *Getting into Oxford & Cambridge 2014 Entry*, Trotman, www.trotman.co.uk.
- *Getting into the UK's Best Universities & Courses*, Trotman, www.trotman.co.uk.
- *Getting into Veterinary School*, Trotman, www.trotman.co.uk.
- *Getting into Nursing & Midwifery Courses*, Trotman, www.trotman.co.uk.
- *Insider's Guide to Applying to University*, Trotman, www.trotman.co.uk.
- *The UCAS Guide to Getting into University and College*, UCAS, www.ucasbooks.com.

Websites

- www.cam.ac.uk: for information on applications to Cambridge.
- www.ox.ac.uk: for information on applications to Oxford.
- www.cukas.ac.uk.

9 | Interviews and selection

In many cases, the decision to offer you a place will be made using the information you supplied on your application, but admissions tutors for several courses often require more detailed information about applicants. If this applies to you, you can expect to be asked to attend an interview or audition, or to take a written test.

Interviews

Many universities and colleges (especially the popular ones, running competitive courses) want to meet applicants and find out whether they would cope with the demands of the course before making an offer.

Admissions tutors are seeking able students with academic potential, in sufficient numbers to fill the places on their courses.

In deciding which applicants to accept, they are looking for the following.

- **Intellectual ability:** Can you cope with the academic and professional demands of the subject and course?
- **Competitive applicants:** How well do you compare with other applicants for the course?
- **Applicants who are likely to accept:** If offered a place, is there a good chance that you will accept it?
- **Students who will make a contribution:** Will you get involved in the life of the university or college and contribute in lectures, practicals and tutorials?
- **Applicants who are likely to get the grades:** Are you expected to achieve the level of grades in your exams that this course generally commands?

And, very importantly!

- **Motivation:** A real and passionate interest in the subject.

They may be able to find much of this information in your personal statement (see Chapter 17), but some will also use interviews to help them decide which applicants to make an offer to. There is usually no standard policy throughout one institution. In most cases admissions tutors themselves decide whom to interview.

In general, interviews are still used:

- for borderline candidates: give it your best shot, because many admissions tutors like to give applicants a chance even when doubtful whether you will make the grade
- for applicants who have not studied the subject before: tutors need to know that you have researched it and know what it entails
- to distinguish between large numbers of similar, very able, applicants: this is particularly likely if you are applying for very competitive courses, for example at Oxbridge or other high-status universities or colleges
- for vocational courses: those that lead to a particular career, for example:
  - dentistry
  - health and social care
  - medicine
  - nursing
  - professions related to medicine, e.g. physiotherapy, radiography, dietetics or occupational therapy
  - social work
  - teaching
  - veterinary science.

The above courses lead to work in a caring profession – which is why admissions tutors particularly need to be able to assess a student's suitability for the career – but it is not unusual for applicants to courses in architecture or engineering to be interviewed, and they may also be asked to take examples of work or to talk about a project.

Universities and colleges that have a policy of calling applicants for interview may arrange to conduct interviews by telephone, video-conferencing or Skype for people who are unable to attend personally. This applies mainly to applicants who live outside the UK.

What will you be asked?

Interviews can take different forms – you could find yourself on your own in front of just one person or an interview panel; or in a group, being observed as you discuss a topic or carry out a particular task. You may even be asked to take a written test.

Interview questions can be wide-ranging and unpredictable – but, on the other hand, there are a few 'old chestnuts' that tend to come up over and over again. It is wise to have considered how you might respond to predictable questions such as these.

- Why do you want to study this subject?
- Why have you applied to this department or faculty?
- Why have you chosen this university or college?

- What are your spare-time interests?
- Why should we offer you a place?
- Have you any questions to ask?

You should also be prepared to talk about the following.

- Your advanced-level study: what particularly interests you? What additional reading and research have you done?
- Topical issues relating to your chosen subject.
- Anything you have mentioned in your personal statement.

In the case of vocational courses, you can expect to discuss anything you have done to gain useful experience, such as work experience in a hospital, care setting, architectural practice, engineering company, accountant's or solicitor's office. Be prepared to describe what you did, what you learned and how the experience helped you to decide on your higher education course.

Preparing yourself

Obviously you should not memorise or recite answers to any of the questions above – but think through the kind of things you would like to say. Taking the question 'Why should we give you a place?' as an example, you could:

- talk about your strengths, interests and ambitions, particularly with reference to courses you are interested in
- mention anything a bit individual or a little different that you can bring to share with others: for example, you may have debating experience, great rugby skills, extensive practice in ornithology or orienteering expertise; or you may have developed mentoring skills through your work as a sixth-form or college ambassador to 11–16-year-olds.

It is a good idea to ask your school or college to give you a mock interview – this can be an excellent way of preparing yourself to think on your feet and answer unexpected questions.

You should start thinking about interviews as early as possible. As you consider your course choices and construct a shortlist of universities and colleges to apply to, you should research answers to the questions admissions tutors might ask. If the admissions tutor comes up with 'Why have you chosen this university or college?', you will then remember their particularly strong facilities or the unique angle of the course.

Try to keep interviews in mind as you write your personal statement (see Chapter 17). It is very likely that interviewers will use this as a basis for their questions, so do not mention anything you cannot elaborate on. Conversely, if you have a particular passion or area of interest in your chosen subject that you are just dying to talk about, make sure you mention it in your statement.

Top tips for interviews

- Dress should be 'smart casual'. There is no need for it to be very formal.
- Make eye contact with the interviewer.
- Do your best to show that you are thoughtful, committed and genuinely interested in your chosen subject.
- Always have one or two prepared questions of your own about the course, opportunities after you graduate or a relevant academic topic. (Don't ask questions only on topics covered in the material already published and sent to you by the university or college.)
- Make sure that you know exactly what you wrote in your personal statement.
- Don't bluff. If you don't know the answer to a question, ask the interviewer to repeat it or put it in a different way. If you still don't know, admit it!

There are further useful tips on preparing for interviews and on what to expect on the UCAS website.

More detailed advice on interview technique and possible interview questions is given in the *Getting into* series (see the 'Resources' section below).

Auditions and portfolios

Your subject teachers will be able to offer more specific advice, but here are a few general points.

If you are applying for a course in drama or music, you will have to attend an audition – usually before an interview. (Some applicants are weeded out at the audition stage.)

Policies vary at different places, but drama applicants can expect to be asked to:

- perform one or more pieces, often one from Shakespeare and one by a modern playwright – at some places, though, you are free to choose your own pieces
- do some improvisation
- do some movement work
- work in a group.

Music students can expect to have to:

- perform at least two (contrasting) pieces – often from a set list but sometimes of your own choice
- sight read
- improvise
- do technical tests (scales and arpeggios).

Art students may have to take a portfolio of work with them – and will be expected to talk about it. The usual advice is to:

- include some work that you have done on your own, i.e. not as part of coursework
- include notebooks and sketches as well as finished work
- bring photographs of three-dimensional work that is too heavy to take with you.

However, some admissions tutors prefer to see portfolios in advance and assess them at the same time as they read the UCAS application. If so, you will receive a request (usually by email) for your portfolio. The email you receive will tell you how to submit your portfolio – and full instructions will be given if you are expected to do so online.

Aptitude tests

Many students now get straight A grades and admissions tutors for oversubscribed courses have no way of distinguishing between them. So several admissions tests have been devised to give them additional information that is relevant to their subjects. The most common admissions tests are for medicine and law, usually the BMAT, the UKCAT and the LNAT.

The BioMedical Admissions Test (BMAT)

This is a two-hour pencil-and-paper test consisting of the following papers.

- Aptitude and Skills: short answers or multiple choice. This is designed to test problem solving, understanding argument, data analysis and inference.
- Scientific Knowledge and Application: also short answers or multiple choice.
- Writing Task: a short essay from a choice of four titles. No prior knowledge is required. You will be expected to develop ideas and explain them effectively.

You must apply to sit the test by the end of September, or up to approximately three weeks later on payment of a penalty fee, and you must sit the test on the one date that is offered in any one year. This is in early November. You may sit the test at your school or college if it is a registered assessment centre or at an 'open centre' (often an independent school that accepts external candidates). There are test centres in many countries.

The cost is £44 (home and EU students) or £74 (international students), with an additional fee of £31.50 for late applications.

You can get full information, including past questions and advice on how to prepare, at www.admissionstestingservice.org/our-services/medicine-and-healthcare/bmat/about-bmat.

UK Clinical Aptitude Test (UKCAT)

UKCAT is a two-hour test consisting of the following sections.

- Verbal Reasoning: designed to assess ability to think logically about written information and to arrive at a reasoned conclusion.
- Quantitative Reasoning: assesses ability to solve numerical problems.
- Abstract Reasoning: assesses ability to infer relationships from information by convergent and divergent thinking.
- Decision Analysis: assesses ability to deal with various forms of information, to infer relationships, to make informed judgements, and to decide on an appropriate response to situations given.
- A fifth section, Situational Judgement, has been trialled in 2012 and may be added. Check the UKCAT website for more details.

All answers are multiple choice.

The test must be taken online at an approved test centre. There are centres in over 160 countries and there are many in the UK, so you should be able to find one within convenient travelling distance.

You may register to take the test from 1 May and there are several test dates between the beginning of July and the first week in October.

The cost varies at different centres: at those in the EU it is £65 if the test is taken in July or August, or £80 in September or October. Outside the EU the cost is £100.

Full information, including a guide to what to expect at a test centre, is given at www.ukcat.ac.uk.

National Admissions Test for Law (LNAT)

LNAT is a two-part online test that takes two and a quarter hours. It is designed to assess powers of:

- comprehension
- interpretation
- analysis
- synthesis
- induction
- deduction.

Section A consists of 42 multiple choice questions based on argumentative passages. Candidates are given 95 minutes to answer all of the questions. For Section B, candidates have 40 minutes to answer one of three essay questions on a range of subjects and demonstrate their ability to argue economically to a conclusion, displaying a good command of written English.

There is no set date for sitting the test, but you may take it from 1 September. Please note that you must first send in your UCAS application since you will need your Personal ID number in order to register. The standard closing date for sitting the test is 20 January, but some universities have an earlier date.

Tests are offered at the same centres providing the UKCAT tests (see above). The cost is £50 at EU centres and £70 at those outside the EU.

There is much more information on the LNAT website, www.lnat.ac.uk, where you can find out more about the different parts of the test and read some tips on both tackling multiple choice questions and writing the kind of essay that will impress.

Can you prepare for BMAT, UKCAT and LNAT?

You cannot learn or revise anything for these tests. However, you can certainly prepare for them by finding out what to expect and practising using practice papers. You should also familiarise yourself with the type of equipment in the case of computer-based tests.

> **TIP!**
> Bursaries are available for all three tests for applicants who would have difficulty in meeting the cost. Full details are on the websites.

Cambridge University

Cambridge uses admissions tests for entry to:

- mathematics (Sixth Term Examination Papers or STEP)
- modern and medieval languages
- computer science, natural sciences, engineering, economics, land economy and politics, psychology and sociology (PPS) at a number of University of Cambridge colleges (Thinking Skills Assessment).

Oxford University

Oxford uses admissions tests for entry to:

- classics
- English
- history
- mathematics or computer science
- philosophy, politics and economics (PPE), economics and management (E&M), experimental psychology (EP) and psychology and philosophy (Thinking Skills Assessment)
- physics.

University College London

UCL uses admissions tests for entry to:

- European social and political studies (Thinking Skills Assessment)
- mathematics (STEP).

University of Ulster

Ulster uses admissions tests for entry to:

- any course including a modern language.

University of Warwick

Warwick uses admissions tests for entry to:

- mathematics (STEP).

Other universities and colleges use entry tests for particular courses. You can find a full list of those that have been declared to UCAS on the UCAS website.

Resources

Publications

- *Getting into* series, Trotman, www.trotman.co.uk. The series gives advice on securing a place at university for courses leading to professional careers (e.g. business, economics and management; law; medicine; psychology; veterinary science; nursing and midwifery) and on gaining a place on courses at Oxford and Cambridge.
- *Getting into the UK's Best Universities and Courses*, Trotman, www.trotman.co.uk.

- *Heap 2014: University Degree Course Offers*, Trotman, www.trotman.co.uk.
- *Insider's Guide to Applying to University*, Trotman, www.trotman.co.uk.
- *Practise & Pass Professional: LNAT*, Trotman, www.trotman.co.uk.
- *The UCAS Guide to Getting into University and College*, UCAS, www.ucasbooks.com.

Websites

- www.admissionstestingservice.org/our-services/medicine-and-healthcare/bmat/about-bmat: BMAT.
- www.ukcat.ac.uk: UKCAT.
- www.lnat.ac.uk: LNAT.
- www.study.cam.ac.uk/undergraduate/apply/tests: Cambridge admissions tests.
- www.ox.ac.uk/admissions/undergraduate_courses/applying_to_oxford/tests/index.html: Oxford admissions tests.

10 | Exam results and afterwards

This chapter looks at what might happen when you have your exam results. However, please don't skip the chapter and think 'I don't need to read this yet!' You might not need any of the information, but then again you might – and panic stations can set in in August. A lot of people whose exam results are not what they hoped for make rushed decisions, leaping at the first option that presents itself. They can live to regret doing so.

This chapter discusses what happens at exam results time and the options you might have if you need to or decide to change your plans. These include:

- Adjustment
- Clearing
- rethinking your higher education plans, perhaps retaking certain subjects or taking different ones
- deciding not to do a higher education course at all.

Before results day

Most applicants are accepted conditionally before their exam results are known, so the results of exams taken or assessments completed in May/June are very important.

After you have taken your exams, you deserve to relax; but it is worth giving some thought to what you will do if you do not get the grades needed for your higher education place – a sort of 'Plan B'. Will you try to secure a place through Clearing (see page 92)? Would you rather retake and apply again next year for the course you really want to do? Or are you having doubts about whether higher education is really for you?

If you are ill or have some other problem that you think may adversely affect your results, tell the universities and colleges whose offers you are holding, or ask your school or college to contact them on your behalf. You may need to get a doctor's certificate to support your case. Admissions tutors will do their best to take such circumstances into account, but they must know about them before your results come out. If you leave it until after you have disappointing results, it may be too late.

> **TIP!**
>
> Always make your application well before the advertised deadline.

Results day

In 2014, A level results will be issued on Thursday 14 August. Results of Scottish Highers will be released in early August (the exact date has yet to be confirmed at the time of writing).

For some qualifications, UCAS will send your results automatically to the universities and colleges where you are holding any offers of a place. Go to www.ucas.com to see the full list of qualifications for which UCAS will do this.

For any examinations that are included in the list on www.ucas.com, you should supply your results to the universities and colleges *only* if they have asked you to do so. However, you can avoid possible delays if you send your BTEC results to them as soon as you receive them. If you have taken any other exams, such as SCE Standard Grade, GCSE or international qualifications, you must send your results as soon as you receive them to those universities and colleges where you are holding offers.

When your results are released and have been received by the admissions tutors, they will compare your results with the conditions they set and make a decision on whether or not to accept you.

> **TIP!**
>
> Arrange your holidays so that you are at home when the results are published. Even if all goes well and your grades are acceptable, you may need to confirm your place and deal with your registration, accommodation and loan. And if things haven't gone according to plan, you need to take advice, find out about course vacancies and make some quick decisions about possible offers of places in the Clearing system.

What if you get the grades?

Congratulations! Your place will be confirmed; a university or college cannot reject you if you have met the conditions of your offer. Before the end of August, UCAS will send you an official notification that your place is confirmed. Your confirmation letter will advise you whether you need to take any further action to confirm your place.

Adjustment

If you met all of the conditions of your firm choice and exceeded at least one, you will be eligible to register to look for another course during the Adjustment period. This begins on A level results day and lasts until 31 August. If you register but do not find an alternative course, you keep your place at your original first-choice institution. In 2012, 1,329 applicants were accepted through Adjustment.

How Adjustment works

Applicants who pass their exams with better results than expected may have not only met but exceeded the conditions of their firm choice. Adjustment gives them an opportunity to reconsider where and what to study.

For you to be eligible to use Adjustment:

- your results must have met and exceeded the conditions of your conditional firm choice
- you need to have paid the full application fee (£12 for a single choice; £23 for two to five choices).

You are *not* eligible to use Adjustment if:

- you are confirmed at your firm choice but did not exceed the conditions of the offer
- you have a confirmed place on a changed course offer
- your original offer was unconditional.

To use Adjustment you will need to:

- register in Track by clicking on 'Register for Adjustment' on your 'choices' screen
- contact a university or college to find another place.

They will check that you exceed the conditions of your firm choice and will tell you if they can offer you a place. You tell them if you want to accept it.

If you are accepted through Adjustment, your Track screen will be updated with the new choice and UCAS will send you a confirmation letter.

> **TIP!**
>
> You can check universities' and colleges' decisions on results day via Track.

If you missed out . . .

Do not panic! You should contact admissions offices immediately to find out whether they will accept you anyway. This is because admissions tutors may decide to confirm your offer even if you failed to meet some of the conditions. It has been known for applicants to be accepted with much lower grades if there are places available, there is good school or college support and, perhaps, a good interview record, although this varies greatly from course to course. But don't count on this, as it doesn't happen very often! Alternatively, you may be offered a place on a different course.

UCAS will send you an official notification of the outcome of your application. If you have been offered a place on an alternative course, you will have a choice of actions. These will be listed on the notification letter.

If your place is not confirmed, you can find a place through Clearing (see below) or, alternatively, you can retake your exams and apply again the following year.

Clearing

If you do not get the grades you had hoped for and your offer is not confirmed, don't worry. If you're flexible and you have reasonable exam results, there is still a good chance you could find another course through Clearing, which helps those without a place to find one. In 2012, 55,721 students found places by using this service. This figure is slightly up on the previous year (51,169).

You are eligible for Clearing if you paid the full application fee and you have not withdrawn from the UCAS system and:

- you are not holding any offers (either because you did not receive any, or because you declined the offers you did receive)
  or
- your offers have not been confirmed because you have not met the conditions (such as not achieving the required grades)
  or
- you made your UCAS application too late for it to be considered in the normal way (after 30 June).

What do I have to do?

You need to search the lists of courses with vacancies to see if there are any that interest you. Course vacancies are published from the middle of August until late September. Arrangements for the publication of vacancies vary from year to year and precise sources of guidance for the summer of 2014 will be announced by UCAS closer to the time. In

2012, for example, official lists of vacancies were published on the UCAS website (www.ucas.com/clearing) and in some national newspapers.

Official helplines are also a useful source of information and advice – try the national Exam Results Helpline on 0808 100 8000, which is staffed by trained advisers.

Make a list of the courses that interest you and contact the institutions, in order of your preference, to ask whether they will accept you. It is recommended that you telephone, email or call in person because the admissions tutor will want to speak to you personally, not to your parent or teacher. Keep your Clearing number (given on Track) to hand as you will probably be asked for it. If you're not convinced that a course is right for you, remember that you do not have to commit yourself.

You need to contact universities or colleges direct about any vacancies you are interested in. If one agrees to give you a place on the course you want, you enter the institution and course details on UCAS Track and they will then be able to accept you. Only when you are certain you have found the right course should you accept an offer of a place. When you have accepted you will not be able to take any further part in Clearing and you will be committed to taking up your place.

Figure 2 on the next page gives tips on what you might do if you do not get a place through Clearing.

Top tips on Clearing

- Talk to your careers adviser about which courses and subjects would be most suitable for you, particularly if your original UCAS application was unsuccessful.
- Remember that you can apply for any course that has places left – you do not need to keep to the same subjects for which you first applied. If you do decide to apply for courses that are quite different from the ones you originally selected, make sure you do your research very thoroughly, referring back to prospectuses and websites. Remember, though, that you will not be able to change your personal statement.
- Although you will have to act quickly, do not make any hasty decisions; accept an offer only if you are sure the course is right for you.
- One way of making sure you are happy with your choice of course is to go to the university or college in person: the best way to find out more is to pay it a visit. Most universities and colleges are happy to make arrangements to meet applicants and show them around, and many will have open days. They know that you could be spending the next three or four years there, and will be reassured that you want to be sure you are making the right choice.

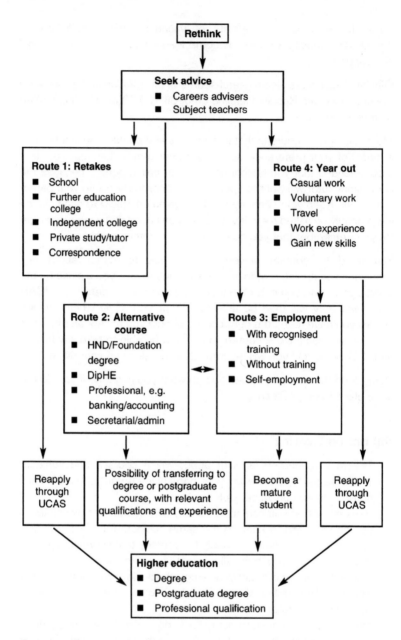

Figure 2 Options after Clearing

- If you are applying for art and design courses, you may need to supply a portfolio of work as well as your Clearing number.
- Remember that universities and colleges are likely to refer back to your UCAS application when deciding whether to make you an offer – you may want to have another look at what you wrote on your personal statement to make sure you are familiar with it, just in case an admissions tutor wants to ask you about it.

Why do you have to wait until August for Adjustment and Clearing?

After all, some people know their results earlier in the year – in June for example.

The reason is that both services operate to fill empty places in universities and colleges. They do not know how many of these they have until the last of the major exam results – A levels – are known. Only then, when they know how many applicants have qualified for places and have firmly accepted them, do they know what they have left.

Some admissions staff may not put their places into Clearing immediately. Why? Because whereas they once had to adhere to rigid quotas and were fined if they accepted too many students, they are now allowed to take as many students with AAB at A level (or equivalent) as they wish. This means that they might wait until they see how many students apply through Adjustment – or even as completely new applicants – before they decide to give places to less well qualified applicants through Clearing.

When you have secured a place through Adjustment or Clearing

Make sure you get from your new choice of university or college the information you will need about:

- accommodation
- term dates
- introductory arrangements.

Some universities and colleges may have sent you this information as soon as you accepted firmly; some only if you asked for it; and a few later in the year (even after your results). Check in good time.

Retakes

Remember, disappointing results need not mean the end of your ambitions. If low grades mean that you have not been accepted on a course of your choice, you could consider retaking your exams.

As this book was being written, the government had announced the abolition of January A level retakes in England from January 2014. Northern Ireland and Wales were holding reviews but had not published their decisions at the time of writing.

- Therefore, in Northern Ireland and Wales in some A level subjects, and with some syllabuses, retakes might be possible in the January following your June exams. However, although all AS and A2 units are set in June, not all are available in January – so you might need to spend a full year retaking and, in that case, you could consider changing to an A level subject for which you have a greater aptitude and a better chance of achieving high grades.
- In England you would have to wait until June to do retakes.
- IB retakes are available in November and May. There are some restrictions so you will need to contact the centre where you might want to do your retakes.
- It is possible to retake Scottish Highers only by waiting for one year. No earlier retake examinations are offered.

While most university and college departments consider retake candidates – and some welcome the greater maturity and commitment to hard work that retaking demonstrates – be aware that you may be asked for higher grades. It is always worth checking with the relevant admissions tutor that your proposed retake programme is acceptable. It is very rare for Oxford or Cambridge to accept applicants who have retaken their exams, for example.

Part III
Using Apply to submit your UCAS application

11 | Introducing Apply

A pply is UCAS's online application system. It is found at www.ucas.com/students/apply. As well as being easy and convenient to use, it:

- speeds up the processing of applications to higher education courses
- incorporates checks that prevent you from making simple errors
- is supported by the very latest UCAS course data and relevant additional information.

This chapter provides a brief outline of the Apply process, giving you guidelines on setting up your account, together with tips on making the application process as easy as possible. The remaining chapters of this book work through each section of the online application.

Getting started

Using Apply via a school or college

Each June, all schools, colleges and careers centres registered with UCAS can access the Apply application system and set it up for the coming application cycle. Your UCAS coordinator will set up a unique password or 'buzzword', made up of at least six letters and numerals, which will be used by you and all other UCAS applicants at your centre so that your application can be identified with that centre.

> **TIP!**
>
> The buzzword allows you to log on to Apply and lets UCAS see which centre you are from. When you enter your buzzword, do not hit the return key. Use the 'Next' button or the buzzword will not be accepted.

You can access the Apply system from any computer on the internet. The first thing you have to do is register. As you move through the registration screens, you will be asked to provide personal details including your first name(s), surname, title, gender, date of birth, address, telephone number(s) and email address, and agree to the UCAS terms and conditions.

Apply will check your details with you (they will automatically be entered into the personal details section of your application, where you will have the opportunity to change them later). You will be asked to choose a unique password and select four security questions with answers. When you have completed the registration section your username will appear on screen. Keep a note of this and your password as you can use these details to log on and use Apply at any time and in any place where there is access to the internet, from Thailand to Tyneside.

After you have registered, the first time you log on to use Apply you will be asked if you are applying through a centre or as an individual.

If you indicate that you are applying through your school or college, you will be asked to enter its buzzword. After you have added your school or college details, your Personal ID will appear on screen – make a note of this as you will need it in future communications with UCAS and with universities and colleges.

Using Apply as an individual

If you want to apply to study on a higher education course but are not attached to a school or college, you can – quite easily from anywhere with internet access – make an application using Apply.

To log in, click on 'Apply' on the UCAS website home page and then select the relevant links. When you have read through the guidance, you can register from the Apply home page. Select 'Register/Log in to use Apply 2014'. You will be asked to choose a password and four security questions and answers. When you have completed the registration section, you will be issued – on screen – with a username that you must note down and keep secure.

After you have registered, the first time you log in to use Apply you will be asked if you are applying through a centre or as an individual. You should choose 'individual'.

> **TIP!**
>
> If you forget your username or password you can ask UCAS to email them to you by using the 'Forgotten login?' service on the Apply login page.

You will then be asked to answer a set of straightforward eligibility questions to start your application. Your Personal ID will then be displayed on screen – make a note of this as you will need it in future communications with UCAS and with universities and colleges.

After this, the only difference between making an application as an individual and making it via a school, college or other UCAS-registered centre is the procedure for providing a reference (see below). You may apply as an individual and ask your old school to supply your reference if you have left recently. To do this, click on 'Options' in the left-hand menu and click on 'Ask a registered school, college or organisation to write your reference only'; you will need to supply the buzzword. When they have added the reference they will return your application to you to forward to UCAS.

Reference

If you are applying through a UCAS-registered centre, you complete all the sections of your application and then send it to your referee to add the reference. If you are applying as an individual with an independent referee, you enter your referee's details in the reference section of your application and then Apply will send him or her an automated email to ask for a reference. UCAS then sends your referee a username and password to enter a reference directly onto your application through a secure website. Your reference must be written by a responsible person who knows you well enough to comment on your suitability for the courses you have applied to. This could be an employer, a senior colleague in employment or voluntary work, a trainer, a careers adviser or the teacher of a relevant further education course you have recently attended. Your referee cannot be a member of your family, a friend, partner or ex-partner.

Because individuals' UCAS applications are sent direct to UCAS after a reference has been provided (rather than to a referee at school or college to forward), it is a good idea to use the 'View all details' function to view your form and print out a copy to keep before submitting it to UCAS.

If you have any difficulties at any stage, there is help in the Apply area of the UCAS website, or you can seek advice from the UCAS Customer Contact Centre on 0871 468 0468 between 8.30a.m. and 6p.m. on weekdays.

Technical requirements

The UCAS application systems are designed to be accessed via an internet-connected computer. They may work on other devices, but their functionality would be unsupported by UCAS.

Browser

To be able to use Apply, you will need access to a suitable web browser. UCAS supports its online application systems on the following browsers:

- Internet Explorer (version 8 or higher)
- Firefox (version 2.0 or higher)
- Safari (on Mac).

The systems may work on other browsers, but, again, their functionality would be unsupported by UCAS. It's recommended that you use a recent version of your chosen browser as older versions may be less secure.

Most web browsers allow you to 'cache' the web pages you view. This means that they will be temporarily stored on your computer. However, in some instances, caching web pages will not allow you to update your data in Apply. To avoid this, select the browser setting that ensures that pages are reloaded every time you view them.

The method of selecting caching options varies from browser to browser. For example, on Internet Explorer:

- choose 'Tools' from the toolbar at the top of the browser
- from the subsequent menu, select 'Internet options'
- click on the 'Settings' button under 'Temporary internet files'
- under the heading 'Check for newer versions of stored pages', choose 'Every visit to the page'.

Your browser must also:

- have 128-bit encryption enabled
- have JavaScript enabled.

Your computer set-up also needs to comply with the following.

- Your monitor should be at least 15 inches in size.
- Your display should be set to at least 256 colours.
- Your screen should be set to a resolution of 800 × 600 or above.

If you are unsure about any of these points, consult your computer manual or help facility.

Navigating Apply

On the registration screen, you can select English or Welsh from a drop-down list. After that, you can use the 'Options/Opsiynau' link in the left-hand navigation bar at any time to change the language.

When you log on, you will be taken to the main Apply screen. Apply is divided into the following sections:

- personal details
- additional information

- choices
- education
- employment
- statement
- reference
- pay/send.

You can access each section by clicking on its name to the left of the screen. There are on-screen instructions in every section, guiding you through what you have to do. If you get stuck at any point, you can access help text by clicking on the 'Help' button or on the question mark next to each section. The text relates directly to the task you are completing at that point. Figure 3 on the next page shows what the 'Welcome' screen looks like.

Some screens in Apply have 'Next' and 'Previous' buttons allowing you to move from page to page. You must use these because the back and forward buttons on your web browser will not be visible.

Every now and then, you may be presented with an error screen telling you that the page hasn't been found and suggesting that you click 'Refresh'. Do not panic; just right-click on the screen and select 'Refresh'. The page should then be restored and you can continue as normal.

You are free to move between sections as you like, leaving them partially completed ('In progress') and returning to them later if necessary. Just tick the 'Section completed' box and then click on 'Save'.

When you click on 'Save', any inaccurate or missing information will be highlighted in green to indicate that it is not yet complete. Even if you confirm that the section is finished, you can still return to it and update it or add extra information if you need to.

Checking the progress of your application

The status of your application is displayed on the left of the screen. It shows whether each section of Apply is 'Not started', 'In progress' or 'Completed'. A red tick next to a section shows that the section is completed.

At any stage while you're using Apply, you can click on 'View all details' to preview or print a copy of your application in a viewer-friendly format. This will enable you to check through what you've done quickly and easily. Any incomplete sections will be highlighted in green.

> **TIP!**
>
> Remember to save all your changes.

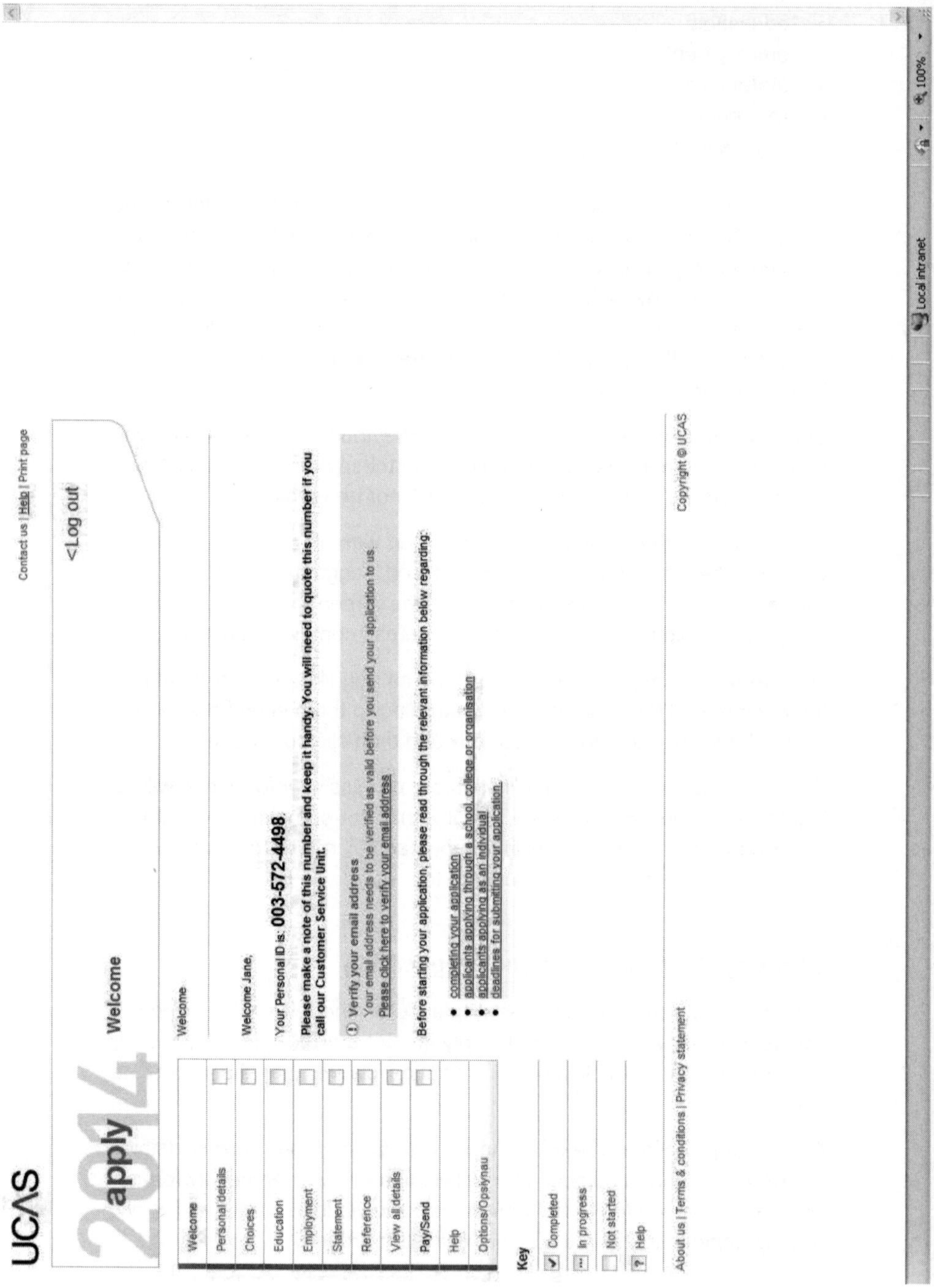

UCAS

apply 2014

Welcome

Contact us | Help | Print page

<Log out

Welcome

Welcome	
Personal details	☐
Choices	☐
Education	☐
Employment	☐
Statement	☐
Reference	☐
View all details	☐
Pay/Send	☐
Help	
Options/Opsiynau	

Key

- ✔ Completed
- ⋯ In progress
- ☐ Not started
- ? Help

Welcome Jane,

Your Personal ID is: **003-572-4498**.

Please make a note of this number and keep it handy. You will need to quote this number if you call our Customer Service Unit.

① Verify your email address
Your email address needs to be verified as valid before you send your application to us.
Please click here to verify your email address.

Before starting your application, please read through the relevant information below regarding:

- completing your application
- applicants applying through a school, college or organisation
- applicants applying as an individual
- deadlines for submitting your application.

About us | Terms & conditions | Privacy statement

Copyright © UCAS

Figure 3: Welcome Screen

You will not be able to submit your application until every section of Apply is complete. Once you have finished your application, agreed to the UCAS declaration and sent it to your referee or asked UCAS to contact your referee, the status of your application will appear every time you log on, at one of the following stages.

- Application not checked.
- Application checked.
- Reference not yet started.
- Reference in progress.
- Reference awaiting approval.
- Application sent to UCAS.
- Your Personal ID is . . .

Once you have submitted your application to UCAS and received your welcome letter, you can use Track to keep up to date with your progress and reply to your offers.

Security tips

For data protection reasons, Apply is a secure area of the UCAS website. More recent web browsers have a built-in feature allowing you to save your password so that you do not have to remember or retype it later. However, if you use this facility it will allow anyone using that particular computer to log on to your account and change the details of your application. For this reason, it is strongly advised that you do not use this feature.

When you have finished a session using Apply, it is strongly recommended that you log out properly by using the 'Log out' button (not by simply closing the window you are in). Once you have logged out you should close your web browser down completely. This will ensure that no one will be able to access your details.

How the rest of this book works

The remaining chapters of this book will take you step by step through each section of Apply, giving you general advice on the nature of the information you are asked for and the basic principles of getting it right. Each area of Apply has a corresponding chapter in this book.

- **Personal details:** basic facts such as name, address and date of birth.
- **Additional information** (for UK applicants only): mostly data for equal opportunities monitoring.
- **Choices:** your selection of universities, colleges and subjects.

- **Education:** your school or college details and exams, past and future.
- **Employment:** any jobs you have held.
- **Personal statement:** the most important section.

In each section, the subheadings relate directly to the headings used in Apply, so you can easily locate the relevant information.

The final part of the book deals with finishing off your application, including information on:

- your declaration: your agreement with UCAS and higher education institutions
- submitting your application
- fee payment
- your reference.

At the end of the book you will find a chapter on troubleshooting (Chapter 19), which will help you solve some of the most frequently encountered problems. Further help is available via the 'Help' text accessible on individual Apply screens.

Stop and think!

Before you start your application, here are some final tips and reminders.

- Make sure you have done all your research thoroughly and you are happy with your choices. If in doubt, take another look at Part I of this book, 'In the think tank'.
- Collect together:
  - your personal details
  - all school or college attendance dates
  - exam results slips and entry forms
  - any employment details
  - details of the higher education courses you are applying for, including institution and course codes (you can find these on the course search tool on the UCAS website).
- Carefully read through the guidance available on the Apply home page.
- Be honest and truthful – you must be able to back up all your statements.
- Do not try to make more than one application in the same year.
- Remember that once your application reaches UCAS, you cannot amend it or add anything to it.

You should now be ready to start your application – read on, and good luck!

12 | Personal details

Obviously, UCAS and the universities and colleges to which you are applying need to know who you are and where they can get hold of you. There is little use in applying if they do not! What is less obvious is that they will need to know about a number of other aspects of your life. This can be for important financial reasons (e.g. in deciding who assesses your eligibility for funding) or to determine whether you require any additional support while studying, for example if you have a disability. Your application will therefore contain quite a lot of information about you, which we will deal with here.

You may already have entered some of it when you registered for Apply – this information will have been transferred into the personal details section of the application, where you can amend it.

Specifically, this section covers the following:

- personal information:
    - name, gender and address
    - preferred first name
    - telephone numbers, email address and date of birth
    - residential category and nationality
- Unique Learner Number
- student support:
    - fee code
    - student support arrangements
- mailings from UCAS
- nominated access
- criminal convictions
- disability/special needs
- Test of English as a Foreign Language (TOEFL) number
- International English Language Testing System (IELTS) number.

Personal information

The information you entered when you registered will have been drawn through into the registration details part of your application. You can edit or alter it at this stage.

Name, gender and address

Whatever you give as your title, name and address will form the basis of your UCAS and university or college record. Although it may sound surprising, every year there are a number of applicants who make elementary errors when entering their own names! The following example is fine:

- Title: Ms
- Surname/family name: Jones
- First/given name(s): Rachel.

The example below, however, will cause problems (and a lot of people do this):

- Title: Mr
- Surname/family name: Robarts
- First/given name(s): Mark Robarts.

Sorry, Mark – but for ever afterwards, you will be Mr M R Robarts to UCAS and the universities and colleges to which you are applying. This will mean that your name will not match your exam certificates, passport, etc., so take care when entering your details. If your name is not easily divided into surname and first names, decide how you want to be addressed and stick to it.

For example:

- Title: Mr
- Surname/family name: Nik A Kamal Hassan
- First/given name(s):

Chinese students, whose own custom is to put the family name first, will normally have to accept being addressed in the Western style – so the following example will appear as C H A Wong:

- Title: Ms
- Surname/family name: Wong
- First/given name(s): Chu-Hai Angela.

It is just possible that universities and colleges may address you as Wong Chu-Hai, but do not count on it. If you have adopted a Western name, feel free to include it.

Preferred first name

If you have a different name you would rather be known as, please enter it in this field. For example, your proper first name is Andrew but you are known as Andy.

> **TIP!**
>
> Do not provide nicknames. It is important that you enter the same names that appear on official documents such as exam certificates.

Gender

For gender, you are asked to choose the option 'exactly as it is stated on official documents, such as your passport, birth certificate or driving licence'.

Address

The address section should not present you with any particularly challenging problems. Your postal address is the one that will appear in the UCAS record, and is where written correspondence about your application will be sent. This does not have to be your home address; you are at liberty to have your letters sent anywhere you choose – your school, for example.

If you do decide to give your school address, you will need to change your address on Apply to your home address, or another more suitable location, once you leave school – UCAS will not do this automatically. You can do this yourself online using Track. (Tell your university or college as well.) If you do not inform UCAS, offers of places or details of Clearing opportunities will be sent to your school. This will mean a delay in you receiving them and you could lose a place as a result.

In all instances, it is very important that you include your postcode as UCAS pre-sorts its letters for the Post Office using the postcode, and correspondence with you might be delayed if you do not put it on your application.

Telephone numbers, email address and date of birth

Include your home telephone number, mobile number and email address if you have them or access to them. Some admissions tutors prefer to communicate electronically, and it can speed up communication dramatically at confirmation and Clearing time.

Make sure you include the area code in your home number, but do not use brackets, spaces, dashes or the '+' symbol. If it is an overseas number, remember to include the international dialling code.

Your date of birth is required for UCAS's and institutions' records: select the day, month and year from the drop-down lists.

Residential category and nationality

Indicating whether your permanent home is in the UK or elsewhere should be straightforward, but your area of permanent residence is less so. If you live:

- outside the UK: name the country (e.g. Australia)
- in Scotland: name the district or islands area (e.g. Clackmannan-shire)
- in Greater London: name the London borough (e.g. Bexley)
- in a former metropolitan district: name the district (e.g. Sefton)
- elsewhere in the UK: name the county (e.g. Northamptonshire).

Apply provides a pop-up list of counties and boroughs for you to choose from if you answered 'Yes' to 'Is your permanent home in the UK?', and a list of countries if you answered 'No'.

Your country of birth and nationality should present no problems, although it is worth mentioning that if you were born in the UK, you should select 'United Kingdom' for the former and 'UK national' for the latter (i.e. you cannot select 'Scotland', 'English', etc.). This information is for statistical purposes only, to find out where applicants come from. It will not be used for selection purposes.

If your country of birth is not in the UK, you will also have to indicate your date of first entry to live in the UK. Using the drop-down lists, you should enter the date when you entered, or propose to enter, the UK.

Residential category can be more complicated, but it is particularly important because what you enter here will be the point from which universities and colleges will start to classify you as 'home' or 'overseas' for the purpose of tuition fees. Those classified as overseas students pay a much higher annual tuition fee. (Your tuition fee status has no direct connection with your nationality: it depends on your place of ordinary residence and the length of time you have been ordinarily resident there.) You must choose from a list of residential category options, summarised below.

> **TIP!**
>
> If you cannot find your area on the list, you need to look through the existing options to find one that matches your circumstances.

UK citizen or EU national

You are a UK or EU national, or are the child or grandchild, or the spouse or civil partner of a UK or EU national, and have lived in the European Economic Area (EEA), Switzerland or Overseas Territories (OT) for the past three years, but not just for full-time education. You also qualify if you have been living in the EEA, Switzerland or OT for three years partly for full-time education, and you also lived in the EEA, Switzerland or OT prior to that three-year period.

EEA or Swiss national

Either: you are an EEA or Swiss national working in the UK, or you are the child, spouse or civil partner of such a person, or you are the parent or grandparent of an EEA national working in the UK. You have lived in the EEA or Switzerland or OT for the past three years, but not just for full-time education. You also qualify if you have been living in the EEA, Switzerland or OT for three years partly for full-time education, and you also lived in the EEA, Switzerland or OT prior to that three-year period.

Or: you are the child of a Swiss national and have lived in the EEA, Switzerland or OT for the past three years, but not just for full-time education. You also qualify if you have been living in the EEA, Switzerland or OT for three years partly for full-time education, and you also lived in the EEA, Switzerland or OT prior to that three-year period.

Child of a Turkish worker

You are the child of a Turkish national who has lawfully worked in the UK, and you have lived in the EEA, Switzerland or Turkey for the past three years.

Refugee

You have been recognised as a refugee by the British government or you are the spouse, civil partner or child aged under 18 of such a person at the time of the asylum application.

Humanitarian Protection or similar

You have been granted Exceptional Leave to Enter or Remain, Humanitarian Protection or Discretionary Leave or you are the spouse, civil partner or child aged under 18 of such a person at the time of the asylum application.

Settled in the UK

You have Indefinite Leave to Enter or Remain in the UK or have the Right of Abode in the UK and have lived in the UK, the Channel Islands or the Isle of Man (or more than one of these) for three years, but not just for full-time education. (However, this does not apply if you are exempt from immigration control, for example as a diplomat, a member of visiting armed forces or an employee of an international organisation or the family or staff member of such a person: if this is your situation, your residential category is 'Other'.)

Other

Based on the answers to the questions in the help text of Apply, you fit into the 'Other' category. You should take extra care that you enter the correct category. The help text in Apply has a series of questions that can help you to choose the right one. If you find this section difficult to complete (if, for example, you live overseas because of your parents' work), classify yourself as best you can and be prepared for questions from the institutions.

They will try to be fair to you, but they do have a duty to apply the regulations equitably to all their students. You could, before applying, write to universities and colleges outlining your circumstances. Some overseas companies have standard letters for employees to use. It sometimes happens that different universities and colleges will classify the same student in different ways, depending on their reading of the rules.

Unique Learner Number (ULN)

You may have a ULN if you started studying for a UK qualification from 2008 onwards. If you have, enter it in the box provided. The ULN should be 10 digits long (i.e. only numbers).

Student support

Use the drop-down list next to 'Fee code' to select which code applies to you. The list below will help you decide which code to choose.

01 Entire cost of tuition fees paid by private finance.

02 Applying for student support assessment by local authority, Student Finance England, Student Finance Wales, SAAS or Student Finance Northern Ireland, Student Loans Company EU Team, Channel Islands or Isle of Man agency.

04 Contribution from a research council.

05 Contribution from the Department of Health or a regional health authority.

06 International student award from the UK government or the British Council.

07 Contribution from a training agency.

08 Contribution from another government source.

09 Contribution from an international agency, government, university or industry.

10 Contribution from UK industry or commerce.

90 Other source of finance.

99 Not known.

Most applicants from the UK, Channel Islands, Isle of Man and the EU will be in category 02. You should use that code if you are eligible for assessment under student support arrangements even if you think your family income will be too high for you to receive support.

If you select fee code 02, there is space provided in the application (under 'Student support arrangements') for you to enter which body will assess your eligibility for funds.

If you are applying for sponsorship, give the name of your first choice sponsor in the personal statement section. You can find out more about company sponsorship from a careers adviser. You should note in the personal statement (see Chapter 17) if you plan to defer to 2015 should your application for sponsorship this year be unsuccessful. For more information on funding and other financial concerns, see Chapter 3.

Mailings from UCAS

From time to time UCAS sends out information not directly related to your application but covering areas of interest such as funding, sponsorship opportunities, health issues, career possibilities relevant to your chosen subjects and offers of goods or services (such as student banking and travel discounts) relevant to higher education.

Please note that at no time are details of individual applicants released to any of the companies wishing to have information passed to you. Such information may be sent by email, text message or post. You should tick the relevant boxes if you wish or do not wish to receive these mailings.

Nominated access

You have the option of naming one person who can act on your behalf regarding your application. It is a good idea to do so, in case of illness or injury, for example. You need to fill in their name and their relationship to you.

Criminal convictions

To help the universities and colleges reduce the risk of harm or injury to their students caused by the criminal behaviour of other students, they must know whether an applicant holds any unspent relevant criminal convictions. This information must be entered in the criminal convictions section of the personal details area.

Relevant criminal convictions are convictions for offences against the person, whether of a violent or sexual nature, and convictions for offences involving unlawfully supplying controlled drugs or substances where the conviction concerns commercial drug dealing or trafficking. Convictions that are spent (as defined by the Rehabilitation of Offenders Act 1974) are not considered to be relevant for most courses (see below), and you should not reveal them.

You must tick the box, however, if either of the following statements applies to you.

- I have a relevant criminal conviction that is not spent.
- I am serving a prison sentence for a relevant criminal conviction.

(If you are currently serving a prison sentence for a relevant criminal conviction, you must also give the prison address as your postal address on your application and a senior prison officer must support your application.)

If you tick the box, you will not be automatically excluded from the application process; however, the university or college concerned may want to consider the application further or ask for more information before making a decision.

You should be aware that courses in teaching, medicine, dentistry, health, social work, veterinary medicine and veterinary science and courses involving work with children or vulnerable adults, including elderly or sick people, are exempt from the Rehabilitation of Offenders Act 1974 and different rules apply with regard to criminal convictions. For these courses the following points apply.

- The university or college may ask you to agree to a DBS check and, if they do so, you must comply.
- The university or college will send you the appropriate document to fill in. Where this document comes from will depend on the location of the college or university you are applying to.
- The information that will be revealed by the DBS check will vary depending on the type of check required. However, it is likely that, for these courses, the university or college will require either a 'standard' or an 'enhanced' DBS check and either of these checks will reveal spent convictions as well as unspent convictions, cautions (including oral cautions), reprimands, final warnings and binding over orders, irrespective of when these occurred.
- This means that if you have a criminal conviction, spent or unspent, this information will be made known to the university or college (but not UCAS) as part of the DBS check.
- If the DBS check reveals that you have had a conviction, caution, reprimand, final warning or binding over order, the university or college will need to assess your fitness to practise in the profession to which you are applying. Applicants to medicine, for instance, need to be aware that the General Medical Council will not permit

students deemed unfit to practise to be entered on the Medical Register, which means that they will not be able to practise as doctors. Similar restrictions might be imposed by other professional bodies, such as, but not limited to, those connected with accountancy, banking, law, social work, teaching and the armed forces.

- You may also be subject to further DBS checks (before and/or after you complete your course) by any prospective employers, who will make their own assessments regarding your fitness to practise in the relevant profession.
- If these issues are in any way relevant to you, you should obtain further advice from appropriate bodies. UCAS will not be able to assist you in this respect.
- You might also be asked to cooperate with other checks that come into force in England, Wales or Northern Ireland at any time during the application process or later. If you are taking a course in Scotland, you will need to comply with any requirements of the Protecting Vulnerable Groups (PVG) scheme that may come into force through Scottish government legislation.

You might find these websites useful:

- www.gov.uk/disclosure-barring-service-check and www.homeoffice. gov.uk/agencies-public-bodies/dbs: England and Wales Disclosure and Barring Service (DBS)
- www.disclosurescotland.co.uk: Disclosure Scotland
- www.nidirect.gov.uk/accessni: Access Northern Ireland.

If you are convicted of a relevant criminal offence after you have applied, you must tell both UCAS and any university or college to which you have applied. Do not send details of the offence; simply tell UCAS and the universities or colleges that you have a relevant criminal conviction. The universities or colleges may then ask you for more details.

Notes

1. Applicants or their advisers who wish to declare additional material information but do not wish to do so in the UCAS application should write direct to admissions officers at the universities and colleges listed on the application or at any other institution considering their application.
2. False information is defined as including any inaccurate or omitted examination results.
3. Omission of material information will include failure to complete correctly the declaration on the application relating to criminal convictions and failure to declare any other information that might be significant to your ability to commence or complete a course of study.

Disability/special needs

Universities and colleges welcome students with disabilities and will try to meet their needs wherever they reasonably can. The information you give in the application will help them do this. UCAS will also use it to monitor progress in equal opportunities in higher education.

If you have a disability, special needs (including dyslexia or another specific learning difficulty) or a medical condition, you should select the most appropriate option from the list below.

● No disability (if you do not have a disability, special needs or a medical condition, select 'No disability').
● You have a social/communication impairment such as Asperger's syndrome/other autistic spectrum disorder.
● You are blind or have a serious visual impairment uncorrected by glasses.
● You are deaf or have a serious hearing impairment.
● You have a long-standing illness or health condition such as cancer, HIV, diabetes, chronic heart disease or epilepsy.
● You have a mental health condition such as depression, schizophrenia or anxiety disorder.
● You have a specific learning difficulty such as dyslexia, dyspraxia or ADHD.
● You have a physical impairment or mobility issues, such as difficulty using your arms, or use a wheelchair or crutches.
● You have a disability, impairment or medical condition that is not listed above.
● You have two or more impairments and/or disabling medical conditions.

Further information on these options is given on Apply.

A space is included for you to provide details of any disabilities, special needs or medical conditions that affect you. Some applicants are reluctant to fill this in – either because they do not want to draw attention to themselves or because they think their chances of acceptance may be adversely affected. This is not the case. Universities and colleges need to know about any measures they may need to take to cope effectively with your needs, and if you supply this information it will help them make suitable preparations so that they can:

● make necessary allowances (for example, they may be willing to lower entry requirements to allow for serious difficulties; they may need to provide you with readers or interpreters, or give you extra time to complete your course)
● ensure that any additional facilities or equipment are available (adapted accommodation, for example).

It is in your interests to give all relevant information in this section. It will not affect the university's or college's decision regarding your suitability for the course.

If you claim special consideration on account of dyslexia, be prepared to provide independent evidence (usually a psychologist's report). Allowances will be made but admissions tutors will need to be convinced that you can keep up with the work required.

Other information

TOEFL number or IELTS number

If you have registered for or already hold either of these English language tests (for international students), enter your number in the relevant field.

Passport details

If you need a visa to enter the UK to study, you are asked to provide the number, place of issue, issue date and expiry date of your passport.

Finally, tick 'Section completed' and click 'Save' to save all the information entered in 'Personal details' before moving on to the next section.

13 | Additional information

This section of the application only appears if you answered 'Yes' to your permanent home being in the UK. It covers:

- activities in preparation for higher education
- whether you have been in care
- parental education
- whether you would like to receive correspondence in Welsh
- ethnic origin
- national identity
- occupational background.

Do not worry about the last three (ethnic origin, national identity and occupational background). This information about you is designed to help UCAS and the universities and colleges monitor applications and equal opportunities, not to inform them during the selection process.

Ethnic origin

You are asked to state your ethnic origin, or the category that broadly corresponds with the origin of your recent forebears. Carefully read the options in the drop-down list, and then select one. The options are:

- white
- black – Caribbean
- black – African
- black – other background
- Asian – Indian
- Asian – Pakistani
- Asian – Bangladeshi
- Asian – Chinese
- Asian – other background
- mixed – white and black Caribbean
- mixed – white and black African
- mixed – white and Asian
- mixed – other background
- other ethnic background
- I prefer not to say.

You must enter one of the options listed, even if it is 'I prefer not to say', or you will not be able to register your application as finished.

National identity

You will be asked to classify your national identity. This is different from ethnicity and nationality and can be based on many things, including, for example, culture, language or ancestry/family history.

You will need to describe your national identity using the options listed below. You can use either one option, for example 'Welsh', or two options if you feel you have dual national identity, for example 'English' and 'Scottish', or 'Irish' and 'Other' if you are Irish with a national identity not listed. If you feel that you have more than two national identities, you should select 'Other' for one or both options:

- British
- English
- Irish
- Scottish
- Welsh
- Other
- I prefer not to say
- Unknown
- Not applicable/not required.

Activities in preparation for higher education

Summer schools and similar courses are held throughout the year and are also known as Saturday university, campus days, summer academies, taster courses and booster courses.

If you have taken part in one or more of these activities (or anything similar), select the relevant option from the list and give more details of what you did in your personal statement.

You can enter a maximum of two activities here; if you have attended more than two, list the two most recently attended, together with the appropriate start date(s). Details of any activities not entered in this section should be explained in your personal statement.

Some relevant activities are listed below.

- ASPIRENorth: promoting greater participation in the north of Scotland. For more information visit www.scotland-aspirenorth.ac.uk.

- Discovering Queen's programme: a widening participation project in Northern Ireland. For more information visit www.qub.ac.uk/alpine/ALPINE/5_2_2_e1.htm.
- FOCUS West. For more information visit www.focuswest.org.uk.
- Lothians Equal Access Programme for Schools (LEAPS). For more information visit www.leapsonline.org.
- LIFT OFF. For more information visit www.lift-off.org.uk.
- Reaching Wider initiative in Wales. For more information visit www.hefcw.ac.uk/policy_areas/widening_access/reaching_wider_initiative.aspx.
- Realising Opportunities. For more information visit www.realisingopportunities.ac.uk.
- Sutton Trust. For more information visit www.suttontrust.com.
- University of Oxford's UNIQ summer schools. For more information visit www.uniq.ox.ac.uk.
- Villiers Park post-16 residential courses. For more information visit www.villierspark.org.uk/student-residential-courses.
- Villiers Park Scholars Programme. For more information visit www.villierspark.org.uk/Scholars-Programme.
- Young Gifted & Talented (YG&T) programme. For more information visit www.cfbt.com/teach/giftedtalentededucation.aspx.
- Other. This category includes summer schools run at Aberystwyth and Swansea Universities for pupils from schools and colleges in Wales, and by the University of Ulster in Northern Ireland under the Step-Up programme and the Science Shop. For more information visit the websites www.aber.ac.uk, www.swan.ac.uk, www.ulster.ac.uk/stepup and www.scienceshop.org.

You will also need to say when and where you went to the summer school. You can say what you learned from your visit in your personal statement.

Care

Universities and colleges may be able to offer extra resources or support, for example with out-of-term accommodation, for those who have been in care at some stage. If you choose 'Yes' in response to this field, you will be asked to say how long you were in care.

Parental education

You will be asked to indicate whether or not either of your parents, or your step-parents or guardians, have any higher education qualifications, such as degrees, diplomas or certificates of higher education. If you are unsure, select 'Don't know' from the drop-down list. If you do not wish to disclose this information, you can select 'I prefer not to say'.

Occupational background

If you are aged under 21, you should give the occupation of your parent, step-parent or guardian who earns the most. If she or he is retired, give their most recent occupation. If you are 21 or over, you should give your own occupation. If you cannot fit the full name or title of the occupation in the box, you can use an appropriate abbreviation. If you prefer not to give this information, insert 'I prefer not to say' in the box.

This information is converted into occupational classifications based on those used by the Office for National Statistics, and will be used to help monitor participation in higher education across all parts of society. Please note that this information will not be released to your chosen universities or colleges until after a decision has been made regarding your application.

Correspondence in Welsh

If you have applied to one or more universities or colleges in Wales and you want them to correspond with you in Welsh, select 'Yes'. Note that you need to do this even if your whole application is in Welsh.

If you write your application in Welsh you will automatically receive correspondence in Welsh from UCAS. Since this section is viewed only by UK residents, other applicants unfortunately do not have the opportunity to use Apply to request correspondence in Welsh. If you are in this position, you need to make requests directly to the relevant institutions.

Finally, tick 'Section completed' and click 'Save' to save all the information entered in 'Additional information' before moving on to the next section.

14 | Choices

This is one of the most important parts of your application, and it represents the culmination of your research into higher education. It is often best to leave entering details of the courses you are applying to until you have completed all the factual information required and worked out your personal statement.

Specifically, this section covers the following fields of the Choices screen (see Figure 4 on page 124):

- Institution code
- Course code
- Campus code
- Start date
- Further details
- Live at home while studying?
- Point of entry.

You are allowed a maximum of five course applications, which should be obvious in light of the space provided. You can apply to fewer than five if you wish, and can add other courses until the end of June as long as you haven't already replied to any offers. If you applied to only one course initially you will be allowed to add up to four additional choices, but only if you pay the difference between the single and multiple application fees (£12 and £23 respectively – see Chapter 18 for more information on payments).

Institution code

To make it absolutely clear which courses you are applying to, you need to include details both of the courses and of the universities or colleges that run them. Apply gives you the option of entering these details using course and institution names or codes. You can either find the relevant code using the UCAS search tool on www.ucas.com or find the relevant institution name using Apply. If you opt for the latter method, click on 'See list'; this will bring up an alphabetical list from which you can select the relevant code(s) by the name of the institution(s) to which you wish to apply.

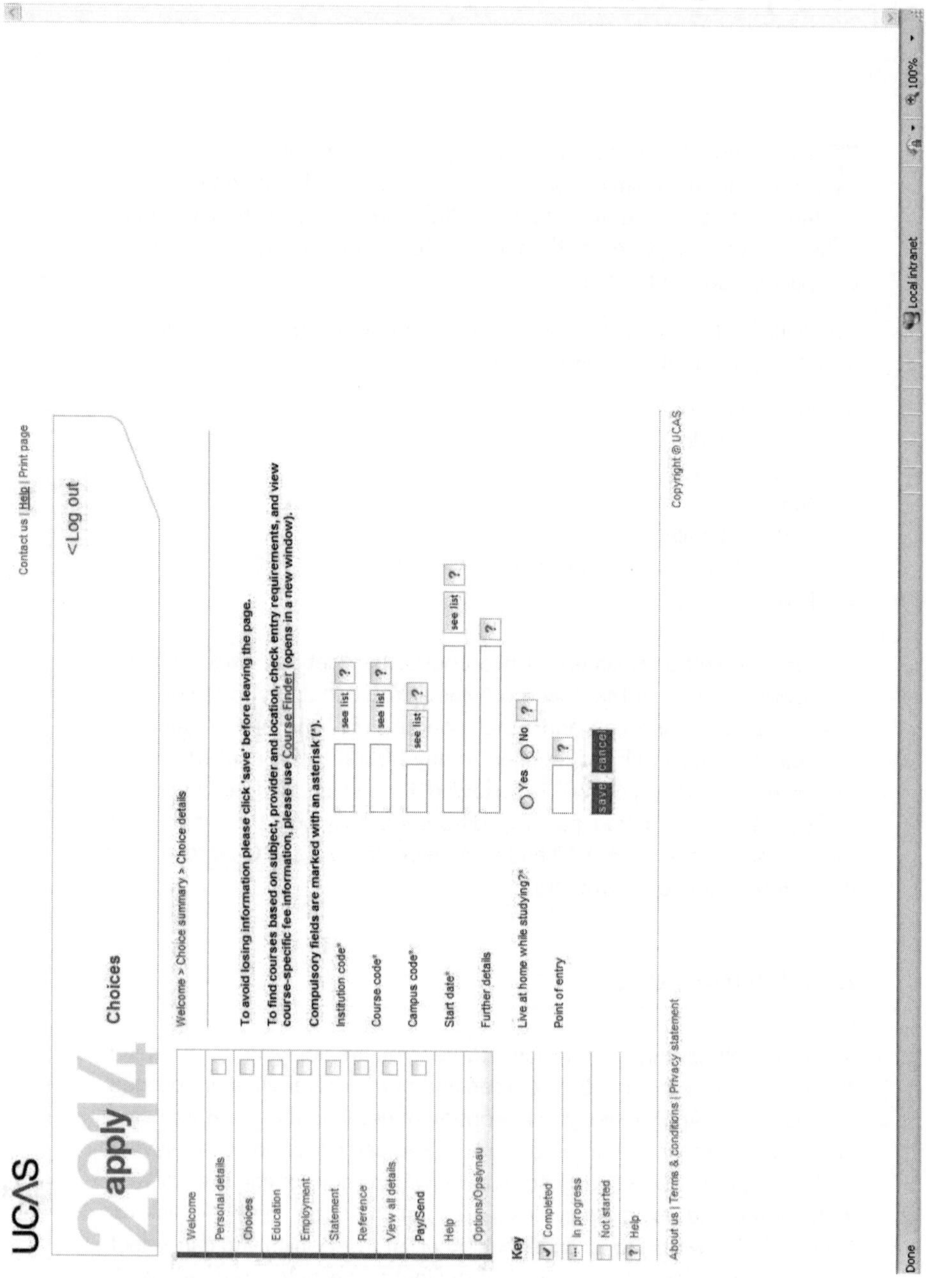

Figure 4 Choices screen

Course code

As before, you can find out the code for the course you wish to apply to via the UCAS website or by clicking 'See list' next to the relevant space in Apply and selecting your course from the alphabetical list that appears (only courses offered at your chosen institution will be displayed for you to select from).

Apply will bring up an error message if you enter a course code that is not recognised, but it is still possible to apply to a course unintentionally if you do not double-check that the code you enter corresponds to the actual course that interests you. Make sure you have access to course information (such as that on the UCAS website) and click 'Save' after each entry. This helps you check for any mistakes.

Nursing and midwifery courses at Scottish institutions, previously applied for through Centralised Applications to Nursing and Midwifery Training Clearing House (CATCH), are now applied for through UCAS. If you select a nursing or midwifery diploma course at a Scottish institution, you will be asked for your National Insurance number and your Nursing and Midwifery Council PIN. Both these fields are optional.

If you select a course that requires applicants to attend an interview or audition or to provide a portfolio or evidence of work, a message will be displayed on screen to inform you of this.

Campus code

Some courses are taught at franchised institutions, i.e. away from the main university or college. If this is the case for one of your chosen courses, you will need to enter a campus code (for example, the Carlisle campus of the University of Northumbria is represented by the letter C), as in Figure 5 on page 126. Enter the relevant code by clicking on 'See list' next to the campus code column. If you are not sure whether a campus code is needed, you can click on 'Save' and see whether Apply highlights the campus box to be filled in. Even if your course is available at only one campus, you may need to select the 'Main' site from the list.

> **TIP!**
>
> Don't forget that you can make insurance subject choices as alternatives to your applications to medicine, dentistry or veterinary medicine or science (see Chapter 8).

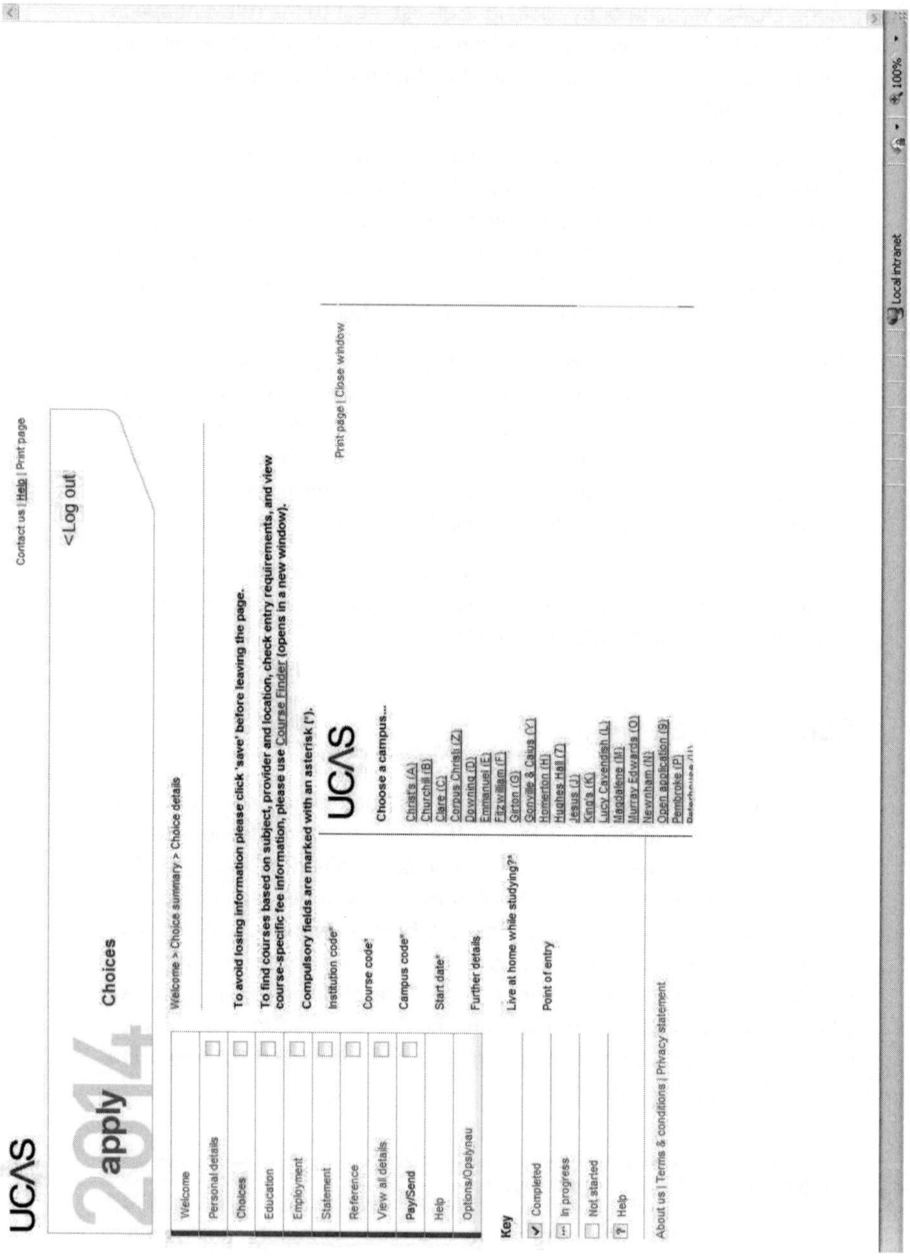

Figure 5 Campus code

Start date

A list of available start dates will be displayed when you click on 'See list'. If you want to apply at this stage for deferred entry (that is, starting your course in 2015 rather than 2014), you should select the correct date from the list. More information on deferred entry is given in Chapter 8. Your personal statement (see Chapter 17) gives you the chance to explain why you want to defer entry.

TIP!

It is no use applying for 2014 entry in 2013/14 if some of your exams will be taken in 2014/15. Even though your start date is deferred, a final decision on this application has to be taken by August 2015, unless otherwise agreed by the university or college. Furthermore, you are not allowed to keep a deferred place at a university or college and then apply the following year to other institutions of the same kind. UCAS has ways of intercepting and cancelling such applications!

Further details

On many UCAS applications this part is left blank. But further information may be requested by institutions and should be provided. Check the UCAS course search tool on www.ucas.com or the university or college prospectus to find out whether this is the case. The sort of information you may need to give could include:

- duration of the course (three- or four-year course)
- minor, subsidiary or first-year course option choice
- specialisations within your chosen course
- Qualified Teacher Status
- previous applications
- if you are applying to Oxford and have selected a permanent private hall (rather than a college with a campus code), this section can be used to state which hall you have chosen.

Living at home while studying?

Choose 'Yes' if you are planning to live at home while attending a particular university or college, or 'No' if you will need accommodation information from the university or college.

Point of entry

If you plan to join the course at the beginning of the first year, leave this part blank. If you think you may qualify for credit transfer or entry with advanced standing (entry at second-year level or perhaps third-year level in Scotland), you should check this possibility with the institutions to which you wish to apply before completing your application. You may then indicate this to the universities and colleges by entering '2' or '3' (i.e. the year of proposed entry) in the relevant box for each application to which this applies.

15| Education

It is essential that you include information about your education to date in your application. This helps to give institutions a better idea of who you are, as well as providing them with evidence of your academic attainment and potential. They will, of course, also use the information you give here to put together conditional offers.

Specifically, this section covers:

- schools and colleges attended
- qualifications (both those already attained and those yet to be taken).

Schools and colleges attended

Apply will ask you to add details of the schools and colleges (including any schools and colleges overseas) that you have attended – see Figure 6 on page 130. You must enter at least one school or college. Click on 'Add new school/college' and use the 'Find' button to search for your institution; the exam centre number will be entered automatically. Higher education and overseas institutions do not usually have exam centre numbers, so if you have studied at one you will need to leave the exam centre number box blank. A warning will appear asking you to enter a number, but you can still move on to the next screen to continue your application.

Enter all the secondary schools, colleges and universities you have attended, up to a maximum of 10. If you have attended more than 10, enter the 10 most recent. If you have spent any time at a higher education institution you must say so, and be prepared for questions about it should you be called for interview.

If you cannot find your school, click on 'My school/centre is not listed here'. You can then type the name of the school into the box.

Select the dates you attended from the drop-down lists. You will also need to enter the exam centre number. You can obtain this from your school or by looking at your examination certificates. If you have been home-schooled for all of your secondary education, click on 'Find' and enter a term such as 'Home'. If a suitable option is not there, click on 'My school/centre is not listed here' and then type 'Home-schooled' into the box.

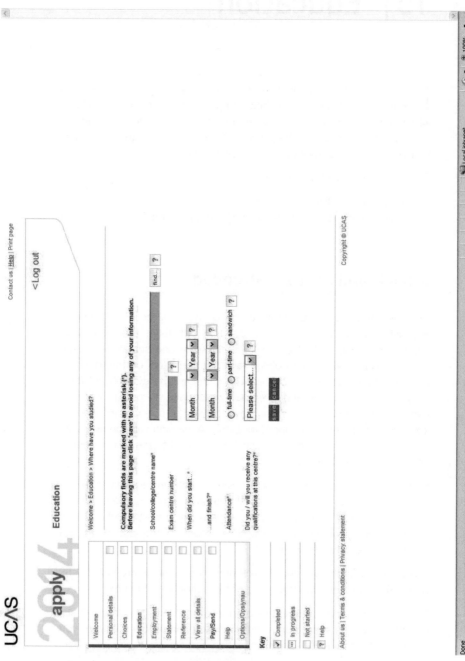

Figure 6 Details of schools and colleges

Qualifications

As outlined in Chapter 6, this part of the application is crucial, as it is bound to be scrutinised carefully by admissions tutors. There are so many different kinds of qualification that you may already have, or may be planning to take, that it is also a potentially confusing area – you need to make sure that you include all the relevant information as outlined below.

Entering your qualifications

After entering the details of the schools and colleges you have attended, you will be presented with a list of them and a link beneath each one to 'Add qualifications'.

Check that everything (dates of attendance, etc.) is correct and click on 'Add a qualification' to enter the qualifications that you took at that school or college. The link will take you through to a list of qualifications that your school or college teaches, for example:

- A level
- A level Double Award
- GCSE
- GCSE Double Award
- European Baccalaureate.

If your qualification is not listed, click on 'Other qualification type not in this list' to access an A to Z list of qualifications. Click on a qualification that you have taken (or will be taking – see below). This will take you to a screen where you can enter all the details of the qualification.

For example, for a GCSE you will need to enter the subject, date of certification, awarding body and grade. If you have not yet completed a qualification, leave the grade box as 'Pending'. You will also be asked to enter information about the units you have taken and unit grades you have achieved in qualifications that have been completed and certificated, such as GCE AS levels. However, entering unit details for GCE AS or A levels is optional.

Once you have completed this screen you then have the option to add another subject for that particular qualification by clicking 'Save and add similar'. When you have no more subjects to add, click 'Save'. At this point, if anything is amiss, you will be told by the green text. If everything is in order, you will be shown the qualifications and subjects you have already entered and given the option to 'Add qualifications'. If you have anything to add, click on this and start the process again.

Once you have entered all the qualifications you have completed or are yet to complete, tick 'Section completed' and click 'Save'.

If you have entered a BTEC qualification or Scottish qualification, you will be prompted to enter your BTEC Registration Number or Scottish Candidate Number in the relevant box. If you do not know your number, ask your college or check your exam certificate. This information could be very important if there is any delay in getting your results to a university or college where you are holding an offer – it could mean the difference between landing a place and losing it.

You can return to the education area of your application, to edit or add to the entries already made, up to the point when you submit your application through your Apply coordinator.

Which qualifications to include?

Qualifications you have already received

You should list all qualifications for which you have received certification from the awarding body (this will usually include GCSEs, Scottish Standard Grades and Intermediate Awards, Intermediate GNVQs and so on). Include all the qualifications you have taken, even if you didn't pass them. You must not conceal anything because you will have to declare at a later stage that you have entered complete and accurate information. You may be asked to supply original certificates to support the qualifications listed in your application at any time during the application process. You must include details of these qualifications even if you are planning to retake, whether completely or only in part. (You can explain your reasons for retaking in your personal statement.)

If you are an A level student, you must include all GCE AS qualifications for which you have been awarded a grade that you have not declined, i.e. all those that have been certificated. You can also include details of your units, and grades if you have them, but you do not have to. If you have opted to decline a result, you should include that qualification in your application only if you intend to retake, treating it as a qualification yet to be taken. You must also include individual units that do not form part of a full qualification (e.g. Free-standing Mathematics Qualification) and for which you have accepted certification.

If you are a mature student with no formal qualifications, enter 'No formal qualifications'. (See page 143 for advice on how you can address this issue in your personal statement.) If you are hoping to enter university or college via APL or APEL, you should contact your chosen institution before applying to UCAS.

> **TIP!**
>
> Mature students should complete this section as fully as possible – many forget to list their present college.

If you are an international student, you need to give full details of all your qualifications in the original language. Do not try to provide a UK equivalent. If your first language is not English but your qualifications were completely or partly assessed in English, make this clear. You should also provide details of any English language tests you have taken or plan to take, giving dates, titles and any syllabus codes. Send a copy of all transcripts, certificates or other proof of your qualifications direct to each university or college you apply to, quoting the title and code number of the course and your UCAS Personal ID. Do not, however, send anything of this sort to UCAS.

Qualifications you are studying for

You must also enter details of all qualifications that you are studying for now and those for which you are awaiting results. These may include A levels, Scottish Highers and Advanced Highers, Advanced Diplomas, BTEC qualifications, NVQs, Access courses and so on.

TIP!

If you have one, you should take your full Progress File (a record of your personal development, skills development and achievements) with you if invited for interview. If you wish, send a brief summary (not the full record) direct to the institution, quoting your Personal ID. You should be prepared to discuss and explain what your Progress File comprises, and how it was developed.

---

16 | Employment

It is very useful for admissions tutors to know if you have had a job or undertaken work shadowing or work experience. This can be particularly helpful if you have worked in an area relevant to your application or chosen career. Full-time and part-time jobs (including weekend jobs) are worth including, but only if they have been continued for a reasonable period. Even if the jobs you held were just to earn pocket money, an admissions tutor will see this as a broadening of your experience. Note that institutions undertake not to contact previous employers for a reference without your permission.

If you have information to enter, click on 'Add an employer' in the employment area of Apply. Then fill in the employer's name (i.e. the company name) and address, your job description, start and end dates, and whether it is/was full or part time. If the job you are entering is where you are employed currently, you do not need to enter a date under 'When did you finish?' Click 'Save' to take you to the employment summary screen and then – when you are ready – tick 'Section completed' and click 'Save'.

If you do not have anything to enter in this section, you just need to tick 'Section completed' and click 'Save'.

17| Personal statement

This section is crucial because it is the only part of the application where you have the chance to select and emphasise points about yourself and to explain to admissions officers why you are interested in your chosen subject(s). Personal statements have a maximum length of 4,000 characters (47 lines) – so you need to think very carefully about exactly what you want to say in the limited space provided. You can click on 'Save' at any time to update the line and character count.

What are admissions tutors looking for?

Factual information

The admissions tutors will want to know about:

- your career aspirations
- your reasons for choosing the course(s)
- relevant background or experience, which may include work experience/work shadowing, practical activity in music or theatre, attendance on courses, time abroad, etc. (evidence of practical experience may be vital to the success of an application to a medical or veterinary school, and may also significantly help your application if you are applying for some management and engineering courses)
- any interests you may have (e.g. Duke of Edinburgh's Award, charity fundraising, painting, potholing, positions of responsibility) – these may not seem strictly relevant to the course, but they help to give an impression of you as a person
- the name of any sponsor you may have. Relatively few students are sponsored through their course and you will not be at a disadvantage if you have nothing to include in this respect. Institutions are keen to know, however, if you have been able to secure this form of financial support. If you have applied for sponsorship but do not yet know whether you have been successful, say where you have applied.

Reading between the lines

Your statement will convey more about you than just the bare facts. The way you present the facts will give valuable clues about other qualities such as critical thinking and communication skills.

Analytical skills

Admissions tutors are usually looking for students who can analyse their current experience. A common weakness is that applicants tend to describe what they are doing now rather than analysing their current experiences, relating them to what they hope to get from higher education and their future career prospects.

Alongside the descriptive approach tends to go a listing of data already entered in the application (e.g. present studies) or details of apparently unrelated hobbies. Hobbies are an important part of your statement, but they need to be analysed in the context of how they have contributed to your skills or personal development in a way that would be an indicator of success on the courses to which you have applied.

Communication skills

The text and presentation of your statement provide the admissions tutor with an indication of your communication skills – both basic grammar and spelling and your ability to express information and ideas clearly.

Maturity

A good statement provides evidence of maturity of thought and a sense of responsibility. If you intend to study away from home, it is important to show that you have these attributes, as they indicate that you will be likely to adapt well to your new environment.

> **TIP!**
>
> It is difficult for an applicant who has selected a wide range of disparate courses to give feasible reasons for having done so, which is why this approach is not recommended.

Top tips

Impression. Think about the impression you want to give – you need to make yourself sound interesting, bright, mature and eager to learn.

Structure. Organise what you want to say into a logical structure and make sure that everything you say is clear and concise. Use subheadings if you think it will help.

Length. Do not try to pack too much in – it can get confusing. Hit the reader with your main point, and do not worry about filling up all 47 lines – rambling on simply to use all the space is likely to be counterproductive.

Relevance. Explain why each point you mention is relevant. Do not unnecessarily repeat material that already appears on the application form.

Honesty. It is imperative that you are honest and specific. If necessary, be selective – there are only 24 hours in a day, and claiming too much is not always a good idea.

Accuracy. Check your spelling. Apply does not have a spell-check facility, so it is recommended that you word-process your statement as a Word document and spell-check it first, then cut and paste it into the relevant Apply area. Get someone else to read it through, too – it's sometimes hard to spot your own mistakes, and computer spell-checkers are not infallible.

Placing 'leads'. Admissions tutors are likely to use your statement as a source of questions if they call you for interview. You should therefore only mention things you are prepared to talk about at an interview. If there is something you would particularly like to be asked to discuss, you can give the interviewer a lead by mentioning it in your statement.

And finally . . .

Check up on yourself. Read critically through everything you have written. Try to imagine you are the admissions tutor, trying to pick holes in what you've said. You may also find it useful to work with friends and read through each other's drafts – you will be surprised how often a friend will say to you, 'But haven't you forgotten . . .?'

> **TIP!**
>
> Save your work regularly to keep the line count updated, and click to preview your statement. Click 'Edit' to make changes, and tick 'Section completed' then click 'Save' to complete.

Creating a winning personal statement

Amazingly, every year there are a few applicants who leave the statement section completely blank. Obviously this is inadvisable, to say the least! But many others do themselves no good simply as a result of the way they present information. The best way to illustrate the pitfalls is by using real examples.

Sample personal statements

Example 1

> Reading, knitting, walking.

Comment

Is this really all you have to say? You do not have to be Einstein to realise that this personal statement is woefully inadequate.

Example 2

> I have been interested in accounting for quite a long time and that's been one of the reasons I took Accounts at GCSE. I was hoping to do Accounts at A level but it was not available at my school. I have had some experience in accounting during Year 10 at school. I found a placement at Electrolux Accounts Department for a week and enjoyed it very much. We were unable to do work experience in Year 12 due to insurance problems. I think the career prospects are good for accounting, with many rewards. I am quite active and enjoy sports like squash, tennis, football and golf. My main sport is golf and I am a member of the local golf club playing off a handicap of 15. I represented my school at golf last year at Seaton Carew and hope to play again this year.

Comment

This was an attempt to do it properly, and there are a few useful points, but the general impression is superficial and negative – it seems that the applicant has simply wandered into accounting as a choice without giving it any serious thought, and the casual tone of the writing does not create a good impression. On the other hand, he or she has at least been specific about their sporting interests: too many people just write 'reading' or 'music'. And it is accurately spelled – these things matter.

Example 3

> At present, I am secretary of the social committee for Years 12 and 13 which arranges social events and also attempts to improve facilities. I have held the position of house captain and also been involved with various sports teams and subject-related clubs.
>
> After abandoning my childhood dream of becoming an astronaut, I became drawn towards the legal profession. Subsequently my work experience in Year 11 was at one of Sheffield's largest solicitors. During the two weeks I was there I spent a brief time in

Commercial, Matrimonial and Police Prosecution departments. All these aspects of law were interesting but my experience in the Criminal Law department was very stimulating and this is the area I wish to pursue a career in – ultimately in the capacity of a barrister.

Outside of school, I am also a member of a sub-aqua branch helping in most aspects of the club, especially the maintenance and administration of equipment and the training (theoretical and practical) of other members. I am a keen cyclist and tennis player and my other interests lie in modern cinema and horology. I also enjoy two part-time jobs where my duties range from gardening, labouring and driving, to shop keeping, stocktaking and the use of an electronic till.

Comment

This is a much stronger statement – note the much more convincing justification for the choice of course; a selector would feel that thought had gone into this. It might have been better to put the second paragraph first – you should try to organise your statement into themed sections covering:

- career aspirations
- reasons for your course choice and interest in the subject
- academic interests
- details of any exam results/achievements you have not entered elsewhere in your UCAS application (e.g. Duke of Edinburgh's Award, Millennium Volunteers, Young Enterprise)
- extracurricular interests and achievements
- work experience.

Example 4

I believe that sciences are the key to the future development of the nation and I intend to be a part of this – that is why I have chosen to study chemistry at university. My passion for science has been reinforced by the work experience I have had in the area: my Saturday job at a local pharmacy made me aware of the enormous amount of research going on into developing new drugs to treat illnesses. I pursued this interest by spending two weeks work shadowing a lab assistant at a major pharmaceuticals company.

During my early school career I held various positions of responsibility: I was my form's representative on the school council for three years and, in Year 11, I was appointed prefect. In the sixth form I have been elected senior student. This post involves many responsibilities, including attending functions such as a meeting with the President of Lithuania. As a student councillor I have been responsible for the production of the annual yearbook. I am also an active member in the college charities group. We have held kara-oke sessions in the lunch hours, and non-uniform days; in total we have raised over £4,000. Outside college I work in a local soup kitchen for the homeless. I have recently been elected to represent the youth of Blackpool on the Blackpool Police and Community Forum. I take an active interest in sports – I am a member of the basketball team, a sport in which I have taken a refereeing course. I was also the school discus champion.

Comment

This example is even tauter, and says everything that needs saying clearly and concisely. This applicant realises that they are applying for competitive courses, and they set out to sell themselves – without going over the top. It would have been even better if the candidate had mentioned something specific that interested them about their work experience or their A level course, as this would give the admissions tutor a useful 'lead' at interview.

TIP!

If you want to supply more information than the statement space allows, once your application has been processed and you have received your welcome letter you can send information directly to your chosen universities or colleges, quoting your Personal ID. (Do not send it to UCAS.)

Specific advice

The personal statement is especially important in subjects such as creative and performing arts. Say what you have done, seen or heard – do not be one of the music applicants who do not actually mention their chosen instrument!

Applicants for teacher training, medicine, veterinary science, dentistry or physiotherapy courses should be sure to give details of work experience (including locations and dates).

If you are currently studying for a vocational or occupational qualification with which admissions tutors may be relatively unfamiliar, explain the relevance of your studies to the course(s) for which you are applying.

If you are an international student, explain why you want to study in the UK. Can you provide evidence that you will be able to complete a course run and taught in English?

If you are a sporting person, give details of your achievements. 'I play tennis' adds little; 'I play tennis for the county' shows that you are committed to something you excel in.

If you plan to take a gap year, it is advisable to cover your reasons for doing so in your statement. Remember that anything you say is likely to be used as a basis for questions at interview. The two examples below show common pitfalls.

Example 1

> In my gap year I hope to work and travel.

Comment

This statement is far too vague and would cause many admissions tutors to wonder whether you had really good reasons for deferring entry, or whether you were just postponing the decision to take up a place on their course.

Example 2

> I have applied for deferred entry in order to gain work experience and then visit New Zealand.

Comment

This is likely to lead to questions such as: What kind of work experience? For how long? Is it relevant to your chosen course? How? Why New Zealand? What will you do while you are there? Try to be as specific as possible. This candidate's statement would have been better if they had explained why they wanted work experience and what drew them to New Zealand.

Mature students

You should say something about what you have done since leaving school. If, like many mature applicants, you are rather older and have had a variety of occupations and experience, you may find the Apply screens too restrictive. In this case you can, if you wish, summarise your career and then send a full CV direct to your chosen institutions (not to UCAS). However, there is enough space for you to present your background and interests in a fair amount of detail.

Everyone's circumstances are different, but the following example is the kind of thing that might attract favourable attention from an admissions tutor.

Example 1

- 1978: Left school aged 16, no qualifications.
- 1979–84: Various periods of travel, manual work and unemployment.
- 1984–92: RAF (included technical training).
- 1992–2005: Self-employed (motor repairs).
- 2006–08: Access course, Silverbridge College (full time) with a view to entering law school.

Most of my experience has been in manual trades, but I now think I have the ability to change direction. I have known many people who have taken degrees and I think I can make a success of it.

My interest in law was awakened by a friend's problem over an insurance claim. I tried to help her and started exploring the law books in the library. I realised that this was an intellectual challenge I could relate to.

Since then I have done more reading and visited the courts. I have started to help in the Citizens' Advice Bureau. Now I want to qualify and I hope to work in a Community Law Centre. My non-academic interests include travel (in various countries), motor car restoration and socialising.

TIP!

Make sure that your statement is all your own work. UCAS will use similarity detection software to check your statement against other statements. If they detect similarity they will inform the universities and colleges that you have applied to. They will also let you know. Each of your universities and colleges will decide independently what action to take.

18 | Finishing off

Declaration

The declaration can be found under the 'Send to referee' section of Apply. Once you have completed all sections of Apply, you need to read the declaration carefully, only agreeing if you are absolutely sure that you are happy with its contents. UCAS cannot process your application unless you confirm your agreement with its terms and conditions, which legally binds you to make the required payment (see page 146).

When you submit your application, there is no need to sign anything by hand: ticking the relevant boxes and clicking on the 'I agree' button suffices.

Remember: by agreeing you are saying that the information you have provided is accurate, complete and all your own work and that you agree to abide by the rules of UCAS. You are also agreeing to your personal data being processed by UCAS and institutions under the relevant data protection legislation. Any offer of a place you may receive is made on the understanding that, in accepting it, you also agree to abide by the rules and regulations of the institution.

To prevent and detect fraud of any nature, UCAS may have to give information about you to other organisations, including the police, the Home Office, the Foreign and Commonwealth Office, UK Border Agency, the Student Loans Company, local authorities, the SAAS, examination boards or awarding bodies, the Department for Work and Pensions and its agencies and other international admissions organisations.

If UCAS or an institution has reason to believe that you or any other person has omitted any mandatory information requested in the instructions on Apply, has failed to include any additional material information, has made any misrepresentation or given false information, UCAS and/ or the institution will take whatever steps it considers necessary to establish whether the information given in your application is correct.

UCAS and the institutions reserve the right at any time to request that you, your referee or your employer provide further information relating to any part of your application, e.g. proof of identity, status, academic qualifications or employment history. If such information is not provided within the time limit set by UCAS, UCAS reserves the right to cancel your application. Fees paid to UCAS in respect of applications that are cancelled as a result of failure to provide additional information as requested, or as a result of providing fraudulent information, are not refundable.

Submitting your application

Once you have agreed to the terms of the declaration, you can pass your application on to your UCAS coordinator or administrator, who will usually be a head of sixth form, form teacher or careers adviser.

They will then check it over, add your reference (see page 147), make arrangements for collecting your application fee and, finally, send it to UCAS.

If you find that you need to alter your application after you have submitted it, you should ask your UCAS coordinator or administrator to return it to you. You will then be able to make the necessary changes before resubmitting it. If mistakes are spotted by the coordinator or administrator, they will return it to you for amendments.

Payment

Application to higher education via UCAS costs £23 (or £12 if you apply to only one course).

If you are making your application through your school or college, they will let you know how they handle payments. (Normally you will pay by debit card, but some schools and colleges prefer to collect individual applicants' fees themselves and send UCAS a single payment covering everyone.) If you are not making your application through your school or college, you will need to make your payment via the internet using a credit or debit card.

You do not need to make your payment until you have completed your application. Once you have agreed to the terms of use of the Apply system in the declaration, you will be asked for your card details (if you are paying by this method). Apply will automatically know whether you should pay the full £23 or the single-choice fee of £12. UCAS accepts UK and international Visa, Visa Debit, Delta, MasterCard, JCB, Maestro and Electron credit and debit cards. At the moment it does not accept American Express or Diners Club cards. The card you use to pay need not be in your own name, but you will require the consent of the cardholder.

If you are applying as an individual but your old school or college has agreed to supply your reference, you can send your application to it. Your school or college will then return it to you with the reference attached for you to submit the application directly to UCAS and make your payment.

Reference

The good news is that you are not allowed to write your own reference, so there is relatively little for you to do here. Your referee (usually a teacher, if you are applying via a school or college) will write it and then attach it to your application, through the UCAS administrator.

Having said this, it is important not to disregard your reference entirely. In some ways it is the most important item in the selection process. It is only your referee who can tell the admissions tutors about your attitude and motivation, and who can comment on your ability, so admissions tutors are not reliant solely on the exam results and information about exams to be taken that you provide elsewhere in your application.

Points of particular concern to admissions tutors include:

- academic achievement and potential
- suitability and motivation for the chosen course
- predicted grades
- personal qualities
- career aspirations.

Referees are asked to estimate your level of performance in forthcoming exams, and these predictions of likely grades are important to your chances of acceptance. The best advice, in this respect, is to work hard and impress your referee! Under the Data Protection Act 1998, you have the right to see your reference. You should contact UCAS if you want to see all the information UCAS holds about you, including what your referee has written about you. You will be charged a £10 handling fee to receive a copy. There is now no such thing as a confidential reference.

Your reference will normally come from your present school or college, or the school or college you attended most recently. If you choose anyone else, make sure it is someone who can provide the kind of assessment higher education institutions need. Be aware that, if you are attending a school or college, it will look very odd if you choose someone from outside as your referee.

What happens next?

On receipt of your application, UCAS will (usually within 24 hours) mail out a welcome letter containing your Personal ID and a copy of the list of your higher education course choices in random order. You should check this thoroughly and contact UCAS immediately if anything is incorrect.

You can use your Personal ID to log on to Track in order to follow the progress of your application. Later in the application cycle you will receive instructions from UCAS that will help you to conclude a successful higher education application. For more information on this and on offers, see Part II of this book.

19| Troubleshooting

Some common problems

I can't log in . . .

If your buzzword or password does not seem to be working, check the following.

- Have you entered the password correctly? Remember that login details are case sensitive – check that you have all the characters exactly right.
- Are you in the student area (not the staff area, which is for your referee)?
- Is your computer properly connected to the internet?
- Are you able to connect to other websites?

If the answer to all of these questions is 'Yes', you may have a problem with your network or internet service provider. Try connecting to the main UCAS site, www.ucas.com – if you can, there may be a problem with Apply and you should call UCAS's Customer Contact Centre on 0871 468 0468.

I've forgotten my username/password . . .

If you forget your username and/or password at any time, click on 'Forgotten login?' and enter the email address you provided on your application. UCAS will then email the details to you.

Once you have successfully logged in, you can change your password, your security questions or language preference by clicking on 'Options/ Opsiynau' to the left of the screen.

I'm locked out . . .

If you attempt to log on five times without success, for whatever reason, your account will automatically be locked. To regain access, you can:

- ask the UCAS administrator at your centre to unlock your account and/or help create a new password for you

- call the UCAS Customer Contact Centre for help on 0871 468 0468
- wait for 24 hours – after which you will be able to try again.

If you close the internet browser window in which Apply is sitting, rather than exiting by logging out, and you attempt to log back in, you will be presented with the message: 'You are already logged in. Please ensure this is your only active session.' Click 'Log in' if you wish to proceed. This is to protect against your application being open in more than one place at the same time. If you click on 'Log in' you will be allowed back into your account.

> **TIP!**
>
> If you leave Apply open without touching it for 35 minutes, it will time out for security reasons and you will have to log in again.

I've pasted my statement into Apply and it's all gone wrong . . .

The default character size for statements in Apply is 12 points. If you have written your personal statement in Word and used a smaller font size, it might not fit when you try to paste it into Apply, and you will have to reduce the length.

You may lose formatting when you paste your personal statement into Apply – you should edit your statement very carefully. You will not be able to use bold or italicised fonts. The character and line count in Apply may be different from those in your word-processing package. This is because formatting characters, such as paragraphs, are counted in Apply but may not be counted in Word or Pages.

I've completed my application and sent it to my referee, but now I want to make a change to it . . .

You'll have to email or personally contact your referee, who can send the document back to you to amend.

> **TIP!**
>
> It's a good idea if you and your group's UCAS administrator develop an email system for alerting individuals that their application has been returned to them for amendment and that they can unlock it again to make the necessary changes. This system can work both ways!
>
> Alternatively, you can go to the 'How to apply' pages in the students' section of the website www.ucas.com.

More trouble to shoot?

Once you start completing your application, you can access help on each screen of Apply. Most difficulties can be sorted out quickly by clicking on 'Help' and following the clear instructions.

And finally . . .

If you feel you need more information on the application process, visit the website, www.ucas.com.

Appendix: A note for staff on Apply

The online UCAS application system, developed over the last few years, affords real benefits both to student applicants and to UCAS coordinators or administrators in schools, colleges and careers centres. Apply is a secure area of the UCAS website and no installation is necessary.

Students can use Apply to complete online UCAS applications at school, home or anywhere with internet access. When they have finished, they can send their applications to you for checking and to have references added, before you submit their applications to meet the relevant UCAS deadline.

The Apply system has dramatically reduced the number of errors made by applicants, as they can access online help at every stage of completing their applications. Poor handwriting is consigned to the past. It is possible for personal statements to be checked and revised a number of times, as the information can easily be amended and kept up to date.

Apply also allows great flexibility in the mode of payment chosen by the centre. The fee payment method is variable and can be changed through the cycle of the UCAS application process.

Notes for UCAS lead coordinators

As the UCAS lead coordinator, you will be posted a unique centre username and password with the June UCAS mailings to schools and other centres. You can then register with UCAS to use Apply – free of charge – by logging in and entering your name, details of your organisation and a unique buzzword of between six and 30 letters and numerals chosen by you, for use by your applicants. The buzzword identifies your centre to UCAS and will enable applicants to link through your centre to register with Apply.

During registration, students are given a unique username. After registration students can enter your buzzword, which will link their application to your centre. This must be written down and kept safe, as you will not know your applicants' usernames. Each applicant chooses a password and four security questions.

As a UCAS coordinator, you will be in charge of staff set-up – registering appropriate staff with individual usernames and passwords. It is a simple task to remove, change or register new staff with different levels of administrative access (permissions).

From the main staff area you can access the following areas.

- **Applications:** shows all the applications being made from your centre, enabling you to view applications and check the progress of individual applications before they are sent to UCAS.
- **References:** where references can be written, read and approved.
- **Link applications to centre:** some applicants register as individuals when they should have registered through your centre. These applicants can ask to be linked to your centre and those who make this request are listed in this section. You can choose whether or not to set up a link.
- **Send to UCAS:** where you can check the status of applications sent to the staff area, methods of payment, individual applicant fees, dates when applications were sent to UCAS and students' Personal IDs.
- **Delete applications:** where you can delete an applicant's record if it is no longer required.
- **Security:** where it is possible to change students' passwords, and where accounts can be unlocked after unsuccessful login attempts.
- **Set-up:** containing all the standard details, your buzzword, chosen method(s) of payment and dates when your centre's applicants will be unavailable for interview, and where you can also register staff members' details and change their permissions.
- **Adviser Track:** all schools and colleges on the UCAS mailing list are invited to subscribe to Adviser Track, which shows your applicants' progress after their applications have been sent to UCAS. Adviser Track gives you access to Applicant Status Reports which allow you to track your students' progress throughout the application cycle.
- **UCAS Card:** shows which of your students have registered to receive a UCAS Card. The list is updated daily.
- **Forum:** where you can discuss all aspects of the application process with other advisers. This is an adviser-only online forum.
- **Options/Opsiynau:** where you can change the language presented in Apply to Welsh or back to English.

The Apply system is a useful administrative tool that can significantly cut the time spent by staff on the annual cycle of UCAS applications.

It is worth gaining the support of senior management to introduce Apply and to train other staff in its use. UCAS offers one-day training sessions for centre staff managing the Apply process. More information about training can be found on the UCAS website at www.ucas.com/advisers/training.